ASK
SUZE®

...ABOUT DEBT

Riverhead Books
a member of
Penguin Group (USA) Inc.
New York
2007

ASK
SUZE®

◆

...ABOUT DEBT

SUZE ORMAN

This publication is designed to provide accurate and authoritative information in regard to the subject matter covered. It is published with the understanding that the publisher and author are not engaged in rendering legal, accounting, or other professional services. If legal advice or other professional advice, including financial, is required, the services of a competent professional person should be sought.

While the author has made every effort to provide accurate telephone numbers and Internet addresses at the time of publication, neither the publisher nor the author assumes any responsibility for errors, or for changes that occur after publication.

Ask Suze® is a federally registered mark owned by Suze Orman.

People First, Then Money, Then Things™ is a trademark owned by Suze Orman.

Certified Financial Planner® is a federally registered mark owned by the Certified Financial Planner Board of Standards, Inc.

The term Realtor® is a collective membership mark owned by the National Association of Realtors® and refers to a real estate agent who is a member thereof.

RIVERHEAD BOOKS
a member of
Penguin Group (USA) Inc.
375 Hudson Street
New York, NY 10014

ISBN 978-1-59448-970-9

Printed in the United States of America
1   3   5   7   9   10   8   6   4   2

Book design by Deborah Kerner and Claire Vaccaro

ASK
SUZE®

...ABOUT DEBT

Taking Control
of Your Money

If you are not in debt of some kind, you're unusual. For most Americans today, debt is a part of daily life. Using a credit card, borrowing for college, applying for a mortgage to buy a house—taking on debts such as these may well be the first experience many of us have with a financial institution. All the more reason to understand and master the dos and don'ts of debt. Until you know how to manage debt, it's almost impossible to save, invest, or build an intimate financial relationship with a life partner based on anything resembling a strong foundation. Until your debt is in control and part of your life plan, you will not achieve financial freedom.

For many of us, credit card debt is a special trouble spot. To put it bluntly, credit card companies are in the business of separating us from our money. They tempt us with monthly offers of "preapproved" cards and, once we've accepted their offers and accumulated a little debt, they know how to lure us into trouble. To take just one example: If you're susceptible to overspending with your credit cards, you may have noticed that just when your "available credit" limit is reaching zero, a credit card company will raise it. "What a thoughtful company," you tell yourself. You may forget that you are paying 11 percent, 15 percent, 20 percent, or more for the privilege of using the company's money. Most of that is pure profit for the company.

In my opinion, credit card debt—in fact, any debt based on overspending—is bondage. It weighs on your spirits, occupies your mind, and backs you into a corner. At worst, it can bankrupt you.

The following questions and answers are intended to help you get and remain free of debt. What I've attempted to do, in part, is to strip debt of its mystique and rob it of its power to inspire fear. No matter the size or the variety of debt, it is always ultimately manageable.

As you'll see below, there are many, many resources for you to draw upon as you work yourself free of debt: agencies to help you break troublesome spending patterns, overcome your debt, and regain control of your finances and your life; counselors and loved ones to support you emotionally; and information, in books and online, to empower you with knowledge. There is much you can do before you reach the "last resort" of declaring bankruptcy, but even if you find yourself in that unenviable position, it is possible—it is always possible—to begin again, to remake your life *your* way.

THE EMOTIONS OF DEBT

Is it ever OK to have debt?
Yes. Debt has a time and a place in all our lives. But the debt you take on must be in alignment with the goals you've set for

yourself. Do you want to pursue a dream of attending college, for example? Then a student loan that will help finance your college tuition is "good debt." What about the mortgage you're carrying on the house you live in, assuming that the house is not beyond your means? That's good debt, too, because it enables you to share in the benefits of home owner-ship and to maintain a safe haven for yourself and your family. What about the loan you took two years ago to help your parents through a rough financial patch or a health scare? Or the car loan you've applied for, assuming you need a car and can afford the payments? In my opinion, all these loan situations are good, worthy, and in alignment with sound goals.

On the other hand, overspending with credit cards to accu-mulate new clothes or furniture, or to keep pace with your friends' spending, is negative debt. It sacrifices tomorrow's needs to today's desires.

How do I know if I'm in trouble with debt?

With the exception of your mortgage and a few other kinds of "good" debt mentioned above, if you can't pay off everything you owe right this minute—whether it's a personal loan or a $3,000 credit card balance—you're most likely in trouble with debt. I know this sounds radical, but it is a very good rule of thumb. Everyone who has massive debt today started with a small balance and monthly payments he or she believed were manageable. But debt is cumulative and habit-forming: Before you know it, you owe more than you can comfortably handle. I have learned that if you cannot pay your credit card bills in full at the end of every month, you may be heading for trouble.

Why is it that so many people get into "bad" debt?

People go into debt for many reasons, but I have often noticed a correlation—an inverse relationship—between self-esteem

ASK SUZE

and bad debt. I call the result your "debt set point." The lower your self-esteem, the higher your debt set point. If you generally feel good about yourself and are living in a responsible way, chances are you don't have a lot of debt on your balance sheet. If you are spending more money than you have, you are probably spending money not only to obtain more goods and services but also to acquire more self-esteem. The less self-esteem you have, the more debt you create.

What exactly do you mean by my "debt set point"?
Think of your debt set point as your own personal credit limit. It's the point at which you are finally willing—perhaps driven—to put a stop to unmanageable credit card spending. Each of us has our own set point. Yours might be $2,000 or $25,000, but the odds are good that you'll know it when you reach it. It's the point at which you decide to stop the downward plunge. It can be a terrifying point to reach, but in the end it is a blessed relief, because it forces you to take decisive, positive action.

Remember, however, that working on eliminating bad debt involves working on the reasons you got into debt in the first place. This usually means bolstering your self-esteem. Remind yourself that you are not a bad person because you have credit card debt. You are simply a person who has managed your money poorly—big difference! Let me urge you to tell someone—someone you trust—about your credit card debt. It is an important step in beginning to deal honestly with your financial situation.

What qualities put a person at risk for trouble with debt?
I have found that people with large amounts of debt often avoid looking at themselves—and their debt—honestly. Some-

times they are people who have problems with impulse control. When they see an item they want, they just have to have it, without regard to whether they need it or can afford it. People who grew up without much money and later earn a comfortable living sometimes spend too much to make up for what they didn't get as children—without realizing what their motive is. People who feel entitled to the good life, or who are subconsciously copying a mother or father who lived beyond her or his means, can be prone to credit card trouble, too. If you feel the need to impress people with what you have rather than with who you are, you are at high risk for credit card abuse. It's worth noting that debt doesn't discriminate; it affects those with money and those without.

The holidays are fast approaching, and I'm starting to feel that typical end-of-the-year anxiety, mostly about the bills that will come swarming in after the new year. Any suggestions on how to rein in my spending?
The holidays can be one of the most tempting times of the year to overindulge—in food, drink, and credit card use. The holidays are also a time when your generosity can overwhelm your common sense. My advice is to be very, very conscious of what you spend money on. Try to plan ahead and get your shopping done early, during the preholiday months and especially during sales. Also figure out, before you hit the stores, how much you want to spend on each person to whom you intend to give a gift; then make it a point not to exceed that amount. If you are shopping in a department store, try to use cash. If you do charge some purchases and are tempted to "spread the wealth" (or debt) among your various credit cards, remember that the interest on department store cards is usually sky-high. Finally, I urge you to think of gifts that aren't expensive, but that still have lasting meaning. The truth is that

most of us cannot remember the gifts we received last year—
no matter how much they cost. Thoughtful, memorable gifts
are not necessarily expensive ones.

CARD BASICS

Credit cards are a staple of modern life, and rightly so. They
allow you a flexible, convenient way to purchase things you
need and want. They also let you make purchases with money
you don't yet have, and that's where things can get tricky. If
you are careful about which cards you carry, their rates and
terms, and how you use them, credit cards can be very useful.

There are three kinds of cards that consumers generally use
to make purchases: charge cards, debit cards, and credit cards.
The following is a brief primer.

Is there a difference between a charge card and a credit card?

Yes. Charge cards don't provide a line of credit the way that
credit cards do; they require you to pay off the entire balance
every month. For this reason, on applications and in the
monthly statements you receive, you will find neither an interest rate charged nor a minimum balance due. In general, you
pay a higher annual fee for the privilege of using charge cards.
Unlike credit cards, they tend to carry no spending limit. A
typical charge card is the American Express card.

Does the lack of a spending limit on charge cards mean that I can go out and buy a $50,000 sports car?

No, it simply means that the charge card company hasn't told
you how much you can spend. If your spending habits appear

unusual, you can count on getting a call from one of the company's service representatives, or possibly finding that your card has been frozen until the company figures out what's going on.

What exactly is a debit card?
Debit cards are not charge cards or credit cards. Like charge cards, they don't offer you a line of credit. Unlike charge cards, they deduct your purchases directly from your checking account. They function very much like ATM cards or personal checks. You can spend only what you've got in your account.

What are the advantages of a debit card?
Debit cards are very convenient. If you have one, you don't have to carry checks or a large amount of cash. Also, merchants who will not accept a personal check may accept them.

Do debit cards have any disadvantages?
Yes. Unlike credit cards, debit cards are not covered by federal regulations that protect consumers in disputes with merchants. Also, many banks charge fees for the use of a debit card, though others don't. Shop around among banks and other financial institutions for the best deal. Be sure to ask whether there's a monthly, annual, or per-use charge for the card, and whether there's any additional penalty for using the card at another institution's ATM. Another drawback: With a debit card, you can't stop payment on a purchase you are disputing the way you can with a check or a credit card payment. A debit card does not help you establish a credit rating. Finally, depending on the state you live in and how quickly you report the loss, a lost or stolen debit card can result in your checking account balance being used up, plus your overdraft protection amount, too.

Will I be charged a fee for using my debit card?

It depends on your bank. Some charge fees on each debit card transaction when you use a PIN. Other banks charge debit card customers monthly fees and/or require you to keep a minimum balance in your account. Before using your debit card, check with your bank as to the charges you may incur for using it.

Do you mean that there's no legal protection for me if someone steals my debit card and empties my bank account?

Well, there is limited protection. According to the Electronic Fund Transfer Act, you have no liability at all once you have reported your card missing. But timing is everything. If you fail to report the missing card immediately—before someone else uses it—but do so within two business days of having lost it, your liability is limited to $50. (The exception to the two-day rule is if you were on extended travel or in the hospital; in that case, you have no liability.) This $50 limit rises to $500 if you do not notify the bank of your missing card within the two business days, but do notify the bank within 60 days of the time your bank statement is mailed to you. The clincher is that, if you fail to report your card missing within those 60 days, your liability is unlimited.

Please be advised that different issuers and different states offer different additional protection. Some banks won't charge you anything in the case of a lost or stolen card. A few states, such as California, Iowa, Kansas, Massachusetts, Minnesota, New Mexico, and Wisconsin, cap your liability at $50. So please check with your state to find out which limits apply to you.

CREDIT CARDS

CREDIT CARDS

Most credit card companies make money in three ways: from the interest you pay on balances due; from annual fees, if applicable; and from fees charged to merchants who accept the card. The first two components, along with a few other privileges and restrictions, have to be looked at very carefully before you decide which card to carry.

All credit cards look the same to me—are they the same?
No. Many credit cards are store- or service-specific cards. Visa cards and MasterCards are what are known as bank credit cards. This means that they are issued by banks or credit unions. Neither Visa nor MasterCard actually supplies the cards you carry in your wallet—banks do—but they do provide support, staff, and infrastructure to the thousands of credit unions and banks that issue the cards. Each bank can set its own credit standards and limits, and offer whatever other advantages it wants to its customers. What's the difference between the two of them? Not a whole lot. Both offer a lot of buying power, and most merchants accept both.

DECIPHERING CREDIT CARD OFFERS

I get many credit card solicitations in the mail offering a "low introductory interest rate." Is this on the level?
Yes and no. Scrutinize these offers very carefully—sometimes when introductory rates are lower, the rates for balance transfers and cash advances are higher; or the low introductory rate may jump by 10 percent or more after a few months. Obvi-

ously, you want to choose the card with the lowest introductory rate, and the longer the low rate lasts, the better. If and when the rate goes up, it may be a good strategy to get another card with a low introductory rate. In any case, if you have good credit, you never want a card for which the normal rate is above 11 percent.

Should I pay an annual fee?

No. In my opinion, no credit card should carry an annual fee. If the card you are considering has one, take your business elsewhere.

Several times a month a credit card offer arrives in my mail stating that I am preapproved. Can you explain preapproval?

"Congratulations, Suze Orman! You're preapproved!" All of us receive such promotions, but they don't mean much. All "preapproved" really signifies is that you have passed an initial screening. What it doesn't mean is that you are suddenly eligible for a $10,000, $15,000, or $25,000 line of credit. You must apply and be accepted first.

Why can't credit card companies commit to their "preapproved" offer?

They're being cautious. A lot of bad things could happen to you between the time you fill out the application and send it back to the credit card company and the time when the company processes your application. For example, you could declare bankruptcy. You could apply for five new credit cards at the same time (this is a red flag for the credit bureaus, which take it to mean you're about to go on a spending spree). Or you could lose your job or your house. The credit card companies know this, which is why they slip in a provision that allows them to deny your application. (Of course, it's in much smaller print than "Congratulations, you're preapproved!")

Are there any advantages to carrying a silver, gold, platinum, or black card?

One advantage (which I don't really think of as an advantage) is that the credit lines on Visa or MasterCard gold cards usually start at about $5,000 and can reach as high as tens of thousands of dollars. Also, these cards tend to offer a lot of customer perks, such as frequent-flyer miles or collision-damage insurance if you use the card to pay for a rental car.

With American Express gold, silver, platinum, and black cards, you'll be sent a complete itemized annual statement at the end of the year, which can be helpful when you're putting your tax information together.

If I need a higher credit limit, is a gold, platinum, or black card the only way to go?

Actually, if you are a big spender and you pay your bills on time, you can maintain a balance on your regular credit card that approaches and sometimes equals the lines of credit that gold or platinum cards offer—and you can avoid paying the high annual fee that some gold, platinum, or black cards charge. If you spend heavily but pay off your balance every month, call your credit card company and ask whether your limit can be increased. If you're a responsible customer, chances are good the answer will be yes.

FIGURING OUT THE ANNUAL PERCENTAGE RATE (APR)

On my credit card statement, what does APR stand for?

APR stands for annual percentage rate and is the fixed interest rate that you will be paying to the credit card company each year for the use of its money. Prorated on a monthly basis, it will be charged to your account whenever you fail to pay off the balance you owe at the end of the month. (The monthly rate is called a monthly periodic rate; to find out your monthly periodic rate, divide your APR by 12.) Sometimes companies quote and charge a monthly rate; if this is the case, multiply that monthly rate by 12 to figure out your APR. Please note that, depending on how the credit card company calculates its interest charges, the amount you pay could be higher than you expect. Please also note that some companies charge a variable interest rate, tied to general market interest rates.

How do credit card companies calculate interest charges?

There are two ways credit card companies compute interest, and one is markedly better for you than the other. The first way—the better way for consumers—is to calculate interest based on your average daily balance, including new purchases. Let's say you charge $1,000 on your credit card for a stereo system. When your credit card statement comes in, you're short of cash, so you pay $500 against your $1,000 balance. When you get your next statement, you will owe interest only on the remaining $500.

The second way credit card companies calculate interest is by means of what is called the two-cycle average daily balance, including new purchases. Take that same $1,000 balance, of which you paid $500. If your credit card company uses the two-month average daily balance method, your next month's statement will show that you owe interest on almost the entire $1,000, even though you paid off $500 of it the month before. Why? Because if you do not pay the balance in full, the credit card company charges you interest on the average daily balance over two months, or two billing cycles, not just one.

To find out which method a credit card company uses, as well as other important information, read the fine print on your application or offer form, especially the "Schumer Box." Credit card companies don't really expect you to read this, which is often tucked away in the lower left-hand corner. But this is what you should read first.

What is the Schumer Box?

When Congress passed the Fair Credit and Charge Card Disclosure Act (which is a part of the Truth-in-Lending Act), one of its requirements was that all costs associated with a credit card be featured prominently on the application or on the offer itself. These costs must also be easy to read—and without a magnifying glass. The box in which these charges are displayed is known informally as the Schumer Box, after Democratic Senator Charles Schumer of New York, who helped push the Fair Credit and Charge Card Disclosure Act through Congress. The Schumer Box contains information that you should consider carefully before deciding to apply for any credit card, including information about late fees and cash advances.

GRACE PERIODS AND LATE FEES

My credit card application mentions a "grace period." What is this?

The grace period is the time between the closing date of your billing cycle and the date you have to pay your balance in full. No interest is charged during this period. However, with a few exceptions, this grace period applies only if you are not already carrying an account balance. If you are carrying a balance at the end of the month, the grace period does not apply to you.

You will owe interest—starting immediately—on any new purchase you make, as well as on your outstanding balance.

What are late fees?

Late fees are charged if you fail to make at least the minimum required payment before the grace period ends. These can add up, though each company's policy is different. Some companies start the clock ticking if your payment is only one day late; others give you a week or two, sometimes more, before imposing a fee. (Interest charges begin immediately.) Remember, the companies require that your payment be received—not postmarked—by a certain date. You have to take into account the time the mail takes to be delivered, so send in your payment early.

How much are late fees, generally?

In general, late fees range from $35 to $39, and in some cases kick in the day after payment is due. This can add a hefty premium to your account.

Will my credit card payment be credited to my account on the day the credit card company receives it?

Although the Fair Credit Billing Act (FCBA) requires credit card companies to credit your payment on the day it is received, companies seem to set their own specific payment guidelines and get away with it. Some companies take as many as five days to credit your account with a payment. Again, take time to read the small print on the application.

MINIMUM PAYMENTS

How is the minimum payment I have to make on my balance every month calculated?

The minimum must be enough to pay all the fees and interest charges for that month, and at least 1 percent of the principal amount. Depending on your agreement with your credit card company, your minimum monthly payment will range from 1 percent to 3 percent of your balance, plus those fees and finance charges. Actually, you want the figure to be higher rather than lower, because if you tend to pay only the minimum each month, the lower your required payment, the longer it will take you to pay off your debt and, as credit card companies well know, the more expensive that debt will be over the long run. I'll say it now and I'll say it later: It's absolutely essential that you pay more than the minimum amount required each month if you want to get out of debt in a timely and cost-effective manner.

CASH ADVANCES

Is there any difference between charging an item on a credit card and taking a cash advance?

There can be a big difference. The fees and interest rate charged for cash advances can be much higher than those charged for making purchases, so be very careful with cash advances. Even if your basic introductory interest rate is 5.9 percent and you don't owe a balance, many credit card companies charge an additional flat percentage (for example, 3.0 percent) on each cash advance, with a maximum fee of up to $50, and some companies may charge you an interest rate of 18 percent or more on your cash advance.

CONVENIENCE CHECKS

Last year, around the holidays, my credit card company sent me a pack of "convenience checks." Should I use them?

You should use so-called convenience checks only if you are prepared to pay exorbitant interest rates. Call your card company, ask what the interest rate is, and if you don't like it, tear up the checks. These checks are usually "convenient" only for the card companies.

EXCEEDING YOUR CREDIT LIMIT

What if one month I go over my credit limit by accident?

You will be charged from $35 to $39 for exceeding your credit limit. Also, if you exceed your limit, the credit card company may have the right to change the good introductory rate you are enjoying to a significantly higher rate. So there is more than one reason not to go over your credit limit.

ANNUAL FEES AND INTEREST RATES

I don't carry a balance, but all of a sudden my credit card company has begun charging me an annual fee. Why?

Being a "good" customer—paying your bills on time and in full—is not what credit card companies want of you. As far as they're concerned, a "good" customer carries the maximum permissible debt and makes interest payments over a number of months, preferably years. Some credit card companies are beginning to charge an extra fee to those responsible customers who don't carry a balance from one month to the next.

This is perfectly legal, so it's your responsibility to keep on top of any changes your credit card company makes in its rules and regulations. For example, a friend of mine who usually carries a monthly balance received notice in the mail that his card company was changing the way it computed interest, from the average daily balance method to the two-cycle method, including new purchases. My friend didn't have to think twice—he changed cards.

I just got an offer in the mail for a credit card with "zero percent financing for nine months." Should I go for it?

First, be sure you understand what the zero percent financing applies to: balance transfers, new purchases, cash advances, or all of the above? Once you understand this, and if you can really pay off all you owe on this credit card in nine months, then the card will cost you nothing. What the credit card company is banking on, however, is that in nine months you won't be able to pay your balance—at which time you will probably get socked with an interest rate in the upper teens or low 20s. Before you accept such an offer, be honest with yourself about when you'll be able to pay off your debt, and be sure you know what your interest rate will be after the "zero percent financing" period is up.

My credit card company just raised my interest rate for no apparent reason. Is this allowed?

Believe it or not, the answer is yes. The expression "fixed rate" means very little to a credit card company—legally, the company merely has to notify you in writing of a hike in the interest rate 15 days before the increase takes effect. Furthermore, it can then apply the new, higher rate to your outstanding balance. As a consumer dealing with credit card companies, you're usually in the position of "take it or leave it." I would leave it, if I could, and switch to a better credit card.

SWITCHING CREDIT CARDS

If I carry a balance, under what circumstances should I consider switching credit cards?

Consider switching if your interest rate has been raised, the company is using the two-billing-cycle method to calculate interest, your grace period has been shortened, or you're being asked to pay an annual fee. If you're a heavy user with a good credit history, credit card companies are competing with one another for your business, and they will make it amazingly easy for you to switch. But watch your step: Too-good-to-be-true offers usually are. Do your homework to make sure you really are getting the best deal out there.

A very good way to identify the best credit card offers is by checking my website, *www.suzeorman.com,* or comparing current offers at *www.bankrate.com.* If you do not have a computer, then look in this month's issue of *SmartMoney* magazine.

Please note: To keep getting the best deal available, you may have to transfer your card balances two or three times a year. Too much trouble? Hardly. It's only a few calls and 15 minutes of paperwork a year, and it might save you hundreds of dollars. When can you stop being so vigilant? When your debt is gone and you've taken the steps to guarantee that it won't mount up again.

CREDIT INSURANCE

I got an offer from a credit card company for credit insurance. Does this offer me protection from a credit disaster?

Typically, credit card companies like to offer four kinds of credit insurance. Credit property insurance protects you against damage to any property that is securing your loan; credit life insurance promises that if you die, your outstanding balance will be paid; credit disability insurance buffers you against a disabling illness or accident that would keep you from working (the companies usually provide a complete list of disabilities covered); and involuntary loss of income insurance protects against your losing your job or getting fired.

In my opinion, credit insurance isn't worth it, particularly because it is very expensive. If you want insurance, take out a general plan from a regular insurance company that covers some, if not all, of the above.

CREDIT CARD ERRORS

Errors are more common than you might imagine. I'd say that roughly 75 percent of all the people I know have stories to tell about erroneous charges on their monthly statements. You should review your monthly statements carefully. Here are some of the things you may find:

- Your statement lists a charge you don't recognize and certainly didn't make.
- Your statement shows a charge for theater tickets or airplane tickets that you didn't receive.
- You returned an item to a store but it's not reflected on the statement.
- You didn't receive your statement one month—even though it's been delivered to the same address for years—and suddenly you're being charged a delinquency fee or finance charge for failing to make a payment.

If one of these errors, or any other, appears on your credit card statement, by law you are permitted to withhold payment on that particular charge.

If I find an error on my card, what should I do first?

Call the number listed on your statement, report the error, and then immediately put your complaint in writing. The Fair Credit Billing Act (FCBA) says that all inquiries about billing errors must be made in writing and no later than 60 days from the date of the mistaken or disputed charge, or from the date your faulty credit card statement was mailed to you—not from the date you received it. (The 60-day rule covers, among other things, erroneous charges for items you refuse because you did not order them, deliveries to the wrong address, and late deliveries.) Your letter to the credit card company should contain all pertinent identifying information, including your name, address, and account number, as well as a full description of the error in question, including the date of the erroneous charge and the reason you believe it is incorrect.

By the way, always, *always* keep a copy of any correspondence you send to a financial institution, whether it's a bank, a credit union, or a credit card company. Your letter should be typed or word processed, not written by hand. Send it by certified mail, return receipt requested, and make sure you send it to the proper address, which is usually different from the address to which you send payments. (Remember that this is a billing inquiry, not a payment, and you don't want your letter to get lost in the shuffle.) On your statement you will often see a phone number and address specifically for billing inquiries.

Once you've written your letter, you can sit back and allow the credit card company, with its enormous resources, to conduct a proper and thorough investigation. Most cases of mistaken charges are handled quickly and painlessly.

If I'm disputing a charge, can I wait until it's settled to pay my bill in full?

No. Although FCBA rules and regulations state that you are not obliged to pay any charge you are questioning—or, for that matter, any interest on that charge—you cannot withhold payment on the rest of your bill. Be sure to pay the other charges. Otherwise, you'll be accruing penalties and interest charges, and will have no recourse but to pay them.

Please be aware, however, that even though you don't have to pay a disputed charge or interest on that charge while you're still disputing it, the credit card company can continue to charge interest against the amount you are disputing. If and when the dispute is settled in your favor, of course, the company must wipe out the interest along with the disputed charge. But if you lose the dispute, you will have to pay the disputed amount plus the interest accumulated during an investigation. So don't argue with a charge simply to postpone a payment that you really owe.

My credit card company says that I have to prove that the charge I'm disputing is wrong, but I have no way to do this. What should I do?

Your credit card company is in error. It is not the consumer's responsibility to prove there was a billing error. By law, the credit card company is allowed two billing cycles or 90 days, whichever comes first, to resolve your problem. Resolution usually happens in one of two ways: Either the company agrees that the charge was incorrect and credits your account accordingly, or you receive a letter telling you that the charge was correct, along with an explanation.

If I don't pay the charge that I am questioning, will this show up on my credit report as a late payment?

Not if this is the first time you are disputing that particular charge and the dispute has not yet reached a stage where the credit bureaus, which may eventually be contacted by the card issuer, have rendered an opinion on whether or not you owe the money. In general, disputed charges do not count as late payments and are not reported to credit bureaus.

What if, after an investigation, the credit card company insists that the charge I'm disputing is correct, but I still disagree? Do I have any way to appeal the decision?

If you still believe that the credit card company is in the wrong and that the charge is unfair or mistaken, you can take the following step. Send another letter—again, by certified mail, return receipt requested, making sure to keep a copy for your files—explaining why you continue to refuse to pay. Typically, you must do this within ten days of the date on the credit card company's explanation of its position on the matter. If you do this, the card company may now choose to report you to the credit bureaus. But if the company reports you, it must inform you of this, telling you which bureaus it has contacted, and must include a notation to the bureaus that you dispute the charge. Alternatively, you can pay the disputed charge (plus all interest charges).

I've heard that if I find unauthorized charges on my credit card statement, I am only responsible for paying $50 per card. Is this true?

In most cases, it is true that the Truth in Lending Act limits your liability for unauthorized credit card charges to $50 per card. To take advantage of the law's consumer protections, you *must*:

- Write to the creditor at the address given for billing inquiries. Make sure you include your name, address, account number, and a description of the billing error, including the amount and date of the error. Include copies of sales slips or other documents that support your position. Do *not* send originals. Keep a copy of your dispute letter.

- Your letter must reach the creditor within 60 days after the first bill containing the error was mailed to you. If the address on your account was changed by an identity thief and you never received the bill, your dispute letter *still* must reach the creditor within 60 days of when the creditor would have mailed the bill. This is why it's critical to be aware of the dates your billing statements are due and immediately follow up when your bills don't arrive on time.

- Make sure your letter is sent by certified mail, and request a return receipt so you have proof of the date the creditor received the letter.

The creditor must acknowledge your complaint in writing within 30 days after receiving it, unless the problem has been resolved. If you have not received an acknowledgment after 30 days, stay on top of them and remind them that they are required to respond within 30 days. The creditor must resolve the dispute within two billing cycles (but not more than 90 days) after receiving your letter.

What if I discover a mistake on my credit card statement two months or more after my statement was issued?

This shouldn't happen to you if you review your statement thoroughly every month. If it does happen, go ahead and dispute the charge in writing, but be prepared to pay some money. Call your credit card issuer and find out what its regulations are. If the cost of investigation exceeds the amount of the charge, you may want to think twice about fighting it.

What about ATM cards? Am I only responsible for $50 if my ATM card was used without my knowledge?

It depends on when you reported your ATM card missing or stolen. Your liability will be limited to $50 if you report your ATM card lost or stolen within two business days after the card is lost or stolen. You can be liable for up to $500 of what the thief withdraws if you report your ATM card lost or stolen after the two business days but within 60 days after a statement showing an unauthorized electronic fund transfer. If you wait more than 60 days, you could lose all the money that was taken from your account after the end of the 60 days and before you reported your card missing. Visa and MasterCard have voluntarily agreed to limit consumers' liability for unauthorized use of their debit cards in most instances to $50 per card, no matter how much time has elapsed since the discovery of the loss or theft of the card.

STOPPING PAYMENT

How do I go about stopping payment on an item that was defective?

The right to stop payment is one of the best protections credit cards offer. There are, however, some important rules and guidelines that have to be followed. You can use your stop-payment privilege only if the defective item cost more than $50. The purchase generally has to have been made within 100 miles of your billing address (though there are exceptions to this rule; inquire with your credit card company). Before you seek to stop payment, you have to have made a genuine effort to resolve the problem with the company that provided the item or service. And you can only stop payment on purchases for which you have not yet paid the credit card company.

What happens when I do stop payment?
The charge will be removed from your bill.

CORPORATE CARDS

I was given a corporate American Express card for business purposes. I left my job before my employer reimbursed me for some of my expenses. Am I liable for these charges, or is my old employer liable?
You may be liable for these charges, particularly if your former employer is disputing any of them. It depends on the agreement you made with your company when it opened the corporate account for you. To find out who is responsible for your charges, call AmEx and ask for a customer service representative, and/or check with your former employer's human resources department.

CREDIT CARDS AND SECURITY

What if I lose my credit card or it gets stolen?
Report any lost or stolen credit cards to your credit card company immediately, and follow up with a written notice, as previously described. In general, it's a good idea to write down the account numbers of all your cards and put your list in a secret spot in your house and/or in a safe-deposit box. Also, be sure to check your cards every now and then to make sure they are all in place.

A friend told me it's not safe to sign my name on the back of my credit card. Do you agree?

I disagree. You should sign the back of your credit card to protect yourself from unauthorized use of your card. This way, a merchant can compare the signature on the card with your signature on the receipt. And what if your wallet is lost or stolen and the cards inside are unsigned? Whoever has stolen or finds the wallet could sign his name on your cards and use them to rack up hundreds or thousands of dollars in purchases. A signed card is not foolproof, but a signature does make it that much more difficult for someone to take advantage of you.

How can I prevent somebody from using my card?

Keep your cards physically secure in a wallet kept well out of sight. And never, under any circumstances, give your account number or any other financial information over the phone unless you are very sure that the caller represents a legitimate business. If you are in any doubt about this, ask for the phone number of the business and call back. Better yet, ask the business to mail that information to you. As a general rule, I would not reveal my credit card number to anyone whom I had not called.

What about entering my credit card number online?

It is not all that difficult to break into a database and steal records. So if you buy online, be sure the website you're using is a secured website that encrypts your data, and that you double-check your statements each and every month, looking for unfamiliar or unauthorized charges.

Are there any specific credit card scams that I should be aware of on the Web?

I would be very suspicious of e-mail claiming to come from

your online service provider that asks you to resubmit your credit card number. If this ever happens, call your service provider at once. Consumers have also been ripped off by websites claiming to be the official homepages of well-known companies. In this scam, a consumer reveals her credit card number in exchange for merchandise. The merchandise never arrives, but the con artist behind the fake Web page now has the consumer's credit card number!

IDENTITY THEFT

What exactly is identity theft?

Identity theft, also known as identity fraud, is when an individual's personal identification information (such as name, address, telephone number, driver's license number, Social Security number, place of employment, employee identification number, mother's maiden name, savings account number, or credit card number) is used without the authorization of that person, to assume their identity for the purpose of obtaining credit, getting credit cards from banks and retailers, withdrawing money from existing accounts, applying for loans, establishing accounts with utility companies, renting an apartment, filing for bankruptcy, obtaining a job, or committing crimes ranging from traffic infractions to felonies. Identity theft is a widespread crime in this country, with an estimated 8.9 million victims a year.

How does the identity thief take my identity?

Unfortunately, it is easier than you might think. Once they have some of your personal identifying information, such as your Social Security number, birth date, address, or phone number, they can call your credit card issuer and ask to change the mailing address on your credit card account. The imposter then runs up charges on your account. Since the bill is being sent to the new address, you may not realize for several months that your credit card is close to being maxed out. Or they apply for new credit with your Social Security number, birth date, and mother's maiden name. They give the creditor a new address, claiming you have just moved. The new cards are maxed out and you don't even know they exist until you review your credit report or you are denied credit due to the unpaid balance on these new accounts. Once the new accounts are maxed out, the identity thief moves on to a new victim.

Where can an identity thief get personal information about me?

The question should be, Where *can't* they get personal information about you? The identity thief does not need to steal your wallet or purse to take your personal identification and credit cards. If you do not shred your mail, bills, credit card slips, and other personal documents, it is easy to "Dumpster dive" in your garbage. Believe it or not, Dumpster diving is one of the more common ways that identity theft occurs. This is why I strongly suggest that you invest in a shredder to destroy any paper that includes any personal information before it is thrown away. Another common method is stealing your personal mail (including bank and credit card statements, preapproved credit and mortgage offers, and telephone bills) by completing a change of address form at a post office to divert your mail temporarily to another location, or by stealing it directly from your mailbox. Additionally, they can fraudulently obtain your credit report by posing as someone who has a legitimate legal right to the information, such as a landlord or potential employer. Once they have your credit report, they have all the personal information they need to assume your identity. Please be especially careful when you receive an e-mail from one of your service providers stating that your "account information needs to be updated" or "the credit card you signed up with is invalid or expired and the information needs to be reentered to keep your account active." Do not respond without first checking with the customer service department of the company to ensure these e-mails are legitimate. Many times the identity thief has stolen the company's logos and incorporated them into the fraudulent e-mail to fool you into thinking the e-mails are official correspondence. So please be very diligent about contacting customer service departments to confirm that the e-mails you have received are authentic before providing any personal information or credit card account information.

I think I may have been the victim of identity theft. What do I do now?

As soon as you suspect that you have been the victim of identity theft, you must immediately contact the three major credit bureaus—Equifax, Experian, and TransUnion—by phone and in writing to advise them that you are a victim of identity theft and to put a fraud alert on your credit profile. Request that a statement be added to your file asking that creditors call you before opening any new accounts or changing your existing accounts, to help prevent additional accounts fraudulently being opened in your name. Please be aware fraud alerts and victim statements are voluntary services provided by the credit bureaus. Creditors do not have to consider them when granting credit.

Next get copies of your credit reports so that you will know the extent of the unauthorized charges. Check the section of your report that lists "inquiries." Where "inquiries" appear from the company(ies) that opened the fraudulent account(s), request that these "inquiries" be removed from your report. To remove the fraudulent charges and the inquiries from your credit report, you will need to fill in a reinvestigation form. Credit bureaus must investigate the items in question within 30 days. In a few months, order new copies of your reports to verify your corrections and changes, and to make sure no new fraudulent activity has occurred.

Once you know which accounts have been tampered with or opened fraudulently, they need to be closed. When you reopen the accounts, use new Personal Identification Numbers (PINs) and passwords. Avoid using easily available information like your mother's maiden name, your birth date, the last four digits of your Social Security number or your phone number, or a series of consecutive numbers. If the identity thief has made unauthorized charges or debits, ask the company to send you their fraud-dispute forms.

If your checks have been stolen, stop payment immediately and ask your bank to notify the check verification service with which it does business. Although no federal law limits your losses if someone steals your checks and forges your signature, state laws may protect you. Contact your state banking or consumer protection agency for more information. You can contact the following major check verification companies directly:

TeleCheck: (800) 710-9898
Certegy, Inc. (previously Equifax Check Systems): (800) 215-6280
International Check Services: (800) 631-9656

To find out if the identity thief has been passing bad checks in your name, call:

SCAN: (800) 262-7771

Finally, file a report with your local police or the police in the community where the identity theft took place. Furnish as much documentation as you can to help the police file a complete report. Be persistent with the police department about getting the report in a timely manner. You will need the police report to correct your credit report and to dispute the fraudulent charges with your creditors.

What if the police won't take a report?

Many police departments are reluctant to write a report for identity theft. But this is a circumstance where you cannot accept no as an answer—you *must* insist that the police file a report. If you get resistance to your request, speak to the head of the fraud unit (or white-collar-crime unit) of the police department in the county(ies) or city(ies) where the fraud accounts were opened. If you still have trouble, call and write to the chief of police.

How do I contact the credit bureaus to report fraud on my credit report?

Call the credit bureaus immediately, and then follow up your request for a fraud alert in writing. Below are the addresses and phone numbers of the credit bureaus to notify them of a fraud situation.

Equifax: To report fraud, call: (800) 525-6285 and write: P.O. Box 740256, Atlanta, GA 30374-0241

Experian: To report fraud, call: (888) EXPERIAN (397-3742) and write: P.O. Box 2002, Allen, TX 75013

TransUnion: To report fraud, call: (800) 680-7289 and write: Fraud Victim Assistance Department, P.O. Box 6790, Fullerton, CA 92834-6790

What can I do to minimize my risk of identity theft?

It's virtually impossible to prevent identity theft, but you can minimize your risk by cautiously managing your personal information. As a first step, several times a year order a copy of your credit report from the three major credit bureaus to ensure your credit report is accurate and does not include any unauthorized activity.

Protect pass codes on your credit cards, bank, and phone accounts. Don't use the same code for all of your accounts. Don't use your personal information, such as your mother's maiden name, your birth date, or the last four digits of your Social Security number or your phone number, as a code. You will find that many companies still use your mother's maiden name or your Social Security number for identification purposes on their applications. Request that they use a password instead.

Never give out personal information unless you've initiated the contact or are certain you are communicating with a legitimate organization. Identity thieves may pose as representatives of creditors, financial institutions, and even government agencies to get you to reveal your Social Security number, mother's maiden name, account numbers, and other personal information.

Outgoing mail should be deposited in post office collection boxes or at your local post office rather than in an unsecured mailbox. Retrieve delivered mail from your mailbox as soon as possible. If you're traveling and can't pick up your mail, put a hold on your mail by calling the U.S. Postal Service at (800) 275-8777.

Safeguard your trash by shredding your credit card receipts, copies of credit applications, insurance forms, physician statements, checks and bank statements, and any documents that list personal information.

Keep your Social Security card in a secure place. Only give out your Social Security number when absolutely necessary.

Request to use other types of identification whenever possible. If your state's driver's license uses your Social Security number, request to substitute another number.

Contact your creditors and ask if you have a choice about how they use your personal information in their account file. If you have a choice, request that your personal information be kept confidential.

Always make sure you know that your wallet or purse is in a secure place, especially at work, and only carry the personal identification cards and credit or debit cards that you absolutely need. Leave your other cards in a safe place at home.

Know the billing cycles of your bills. If your bills don't arrive on time, follow up with your creditors. If a credit card bill is not delivered, this could mean an identity thief has changed your billing address to cover up unauthorized charges on your account.

Beware of promotional offers that ask for your personal information—they may be scams run by identity thieves.

I've heard that I should be especially careful of identity theft on my home computer. How can I protect the personal information I may have stored on my computer?

Home computers can be a gold mine for an identity thief. To keep your computer and your personal information safe, follow the tips below.

- Make sure your virus-protection software is updated regularly. Computer viruses can cause your computer to send out files or other stored information that may contain your personal information.
- Only download files or click on hyperlinks sent by individuals that you know. Opening a file from an

unknown recipient could expose your home computer to a computer virus or to a program that could hijack your modem.

- Use a firewall program as added protection to prevent an identity thief from accessing personal information stored on your computer.

- For online transactions, only use a secure browser—software that encrypts or scrambles information you send over the Internet. Use only the latest version available from the manufacturer to ensure that it has the most up-to-date encryption capabilities. When submitting information, look for the "lock" icon on the browser's status bar to be sure the information you are sending is secure.

- Try to avoid storing any financial information on your laptop. If you have financial account information on your computer, don't access your account with an automatic log-in feature that saves your user name and password. And always log off when you're finished.

- Before you dispose of a computer, delete all personal information. Deleting files using the keyboard or mouse commands is not adequate, since files stay on the computer's hard drive, where they can be retrieved. To make the files unrecoverable, use a "wipe" utility program to overwrite the entire hard drive.

Since identity thieves can get some of my personal information from prescreened credit offers, is there anything I can do to stop having them sent to me?
You can opt out of receiving prescreened credit card offers by calling: (888) 5-OPTOUT (567-8688).

I've heard that the three major credit bureaus share my personal information for promotional purposes. Is there anything I can do to stop this?

You can write to the three major credit bureaus to request that they do not share your personal information. The addresses to write to are listed below:

Equifax, Inc.
Options
P.O. Box 740123
Atlanta, GA 30374-0123

Experian
Consumer Opt-Out
701 Experian Parkway
Allen, TX 75013

TransUnion
Name Removal Option
P.O. Box 97328
Woodlyn, PA 19094

I'm constantly throwing away direct marketing mail that contains some of my personal information. I know I should shred this mail, but is there anything I can do to stop receiving these mailings as well?

The Direct Marketing Association's (DMA) Mail Preference Services allow you to opt out of receiving direct mail marketing from many national companies for five years. To register, go to: *www.the-dma.org/consumers/offmailinglist.html*. The DMA also has a service to opt out of receiving unsolicited commercial e-mail for five years. To access the DMA's online form, go to: *www.dmaconsumers.org/offemaillist.html*. When you register, your name will be put in a "delete" file and made available to direct-mail marketers. However, your registration will not stop mailings from organizations not registered with the DMA's Mail Preference Services.

What about the Do Not Call registry? Can it really stop telemarketers from calling?

The National Do Not Call Registry allows you the opportunity to limit the telemarketing calls you receive. Telemarketers covered by the National Do Not Call Registry have up to three months from the date you register to stop calling you. You may register up to three telephone numbers at one time on the National Do Not Call Registry website, *www. donotcall.gov.* If you have more than three personal telephone numbers, you will have to go through the registration process more than once to register all of your numbers. There is a limit on the number of phone numbers you can register in this manner.

You can also register by phone at (888) 382-1222, but you can only register one phone number each time, and you must call from the phone number you wish to register.

My identity was stolen, and I'm afraid the thief may have gotten a fake driver's license or a nondriver's ID card using my identity. How can I find out?

Contact your local department of motor vehicles *(www.dmv. org).* If your state uses your Social Security number as your driver's license number, ask to substitute another number.

An identity thief has falsified a change of address form and stolen my mail. Is there anything I can do?

The U.S. Postal Inspection Service *(https://www.usps.com/postal inspectors/mailthft/idtheft.htm)* is the law enforcement arm of the U.S. Postal Service responsible for investigating cases of identity theft. If an identity thief has stolen your mail to get new credit cards, bank or credit card statements, prescreened credit offers, or tax information; has falsified change-of-address forms; or has obtained your personal information through a fraud conducted by mail, report it to your local postal inspector. You can locate the USPIS district office nearest you by calling your local post office or checking the list at the website listed above.

An identity thief has withdrawn funds from my brokerage account. What should I do?

If you believe that an identity thief has tampered with your securities investments or a brokerage account, immediately report it to your broker or account manager and to the Securities and Exchange Commission (SEC). You can file a complaint with the SEC online at *www.sec.gov/complaints.html*. Or you can write to the SEC at: SEC Complaint Center, 100 F Street NW, Washington, DC 20549-0213. For general questions, call (202) 942-7040.

I believe my passport was stolen. What should I do?

Contact the United States Department of State through their website, *www.travel.state.gov/passport_services.html*, or call a local USDS field office. Local field offices are listed in the Blue Pages of your telephone directory.

If an identity thief has established phone service in my name and is making unauthorized calls, how do I stop him or her?

Contact your service provider immediately to cancel the account. Open new accounts and choose new PINs. If you're having trouble getting fraudulent phone charges removed from your account or getting an unauthorized account closed, contact the appropriate agency listed below.

For local service, contact your state Public Utility Commission.

For cellular phones and long distance, contact the Federal Communications Commission at *www.fcc.gov*. You can file complaints via the online complaint form, or e-mail questions to *fccinfo@fcc.gov*. Or you can call them at (888) CALL-FCC. Or write Federal Communications Commission, Consumer and Governmental Affairs Bureau, Consumer Complaints, 445 12th Street SW, Washington, DC 20554.

My wallet was stolen, and I'm afraid an identity thief may have my Social Security number. What should I do?
The Social Security Administration of the Inspector General investigates cases of identity theft. If your card has been stolen or misused, contact the SSA Fraud Hotline at (800) 269-0271; fax (410) 597-0118; write SSA Fraud Hotline, P.O. Box 17768, Baltimore, MD 21235; or e-mail *oig.hotline@ssa.gov*. For more information, visit *www.ssa.gov*.

My identity was stolen, and I'm afraid someone has falsified a tax return using my identity. Any suggestions?
If someone has stolen your identity and you suspect tax fraud, call toll-free: (800) 829-0433. Victims of identity theft who are having trouble filing their returns should call the IRS Taxpayer Advocates Office, toll-free: (877) 777-4778.

CREDIT CARD DEBT AND RELATIONSHIPS

I carry a large credit card balance, and I also owe my sister $5,000. Since the card companies are charging interest, is it OK to pay my sister after my credit card debt is paid? My sister never mentions the loan, but every time I see her I think about it.

No, I don't think it is OK. I've seen money damage personal relationships more times than I can count and, although there are occasions when asking for help from a family member or friend is the right thing to do, the debt should always be taken very seriously—for it is a serious matter. Whether a debt is personal or institutional, it is a debt. Even if your sister has loaned you money on indefinite terms, this doesn't mean that you should not be paying her something on the loan. If you pay her just $25 a month, you will feel better about yourself—and she will feel better, too. Remember that self-esteem is a key factor in dealing with debt. The fact that you think about the money you owe every time you see your sister indicates that this debt is affecting your relationship with her.

My wife has admitted to me that she has been hiding $3,000 worth of credit card debt. I'm shocked. What should I do?

Your initial reaction to your wife's disclosure may be surprise, anger, and disappointment, but please realize that by talking about it, she has taken the first difficult, important step in freeing herself—and you—from debt. And please take comfort in the fact that you and she are not alone. Secret debt is surprisingly common.

To your wife and others in her position, I would say: If you are hiding debt of any kind, please do tell your spouse. Debt can't be kept secret forever, and your integrity, self-respect, and relationships with others are at stake. Legally, your spouse shares financial responsibility for your debt. Don't keep him or her in the dark. Together, you can work yourselves free from debt.

If I'm married, am I responsible for money my husband owes on credit cards that are in his name alone, and vice versa?

Personally, I believe that if you are married, you have pledged your support—emotional and financial—to your spouse. Legally, the answer to this question depends on the state in which you live. In many states, you are responsible for your spouse's debt, whether your name is on the account or not. In community-property states such as California, for instance, if the day after your wedding your husband rings up $5,000 in charges on a new Visa card and then cannot pay the bill, guess who is also liable? You are. Be aware that having separate credit cards does not necessarily mean that you and your spouse are not responsible for each other's debt. Check your state's laws. (For more on marital financial obligations, please see *Ask Suze...About Love and Money.*)

In terms of being responsible for a spouse's separate credit card debts during marriage, are the rules different in community-property states and in states without community-property laws?

Yes, they are, and here is what you need to know. If you live in a community-property state (Arizona, California, Idaho, Louisiana, Nevada, New Mexico, Texas, Washington, or Wisconsin), you will most likely be responsible for all the debts incurred during your marriage. There are exceptions, but not many.

I do not live in a community-property state. Am I still responsible for my spouse's separate credit card debts?

Probably not, unless the fine print on the credit card application your spouse signed stated that both of you would be responsible for the repayment of the debt, or unless the debt went to pay for family necessities such as food, shelter, and medical care, or for your children's education.

My wife and I separated recently. Can I legally keep her from using our joint credit cards?

If either you or your wife informs the credit card company that you want to close your joint account, the creditor should close the account. (In that event, neither of you can use the account, but both of you are responsible for the full balance accumulated before you closed it.) First, call the credit card company and ask to have the account closed. Then follow up with a letter. As always, send your letter via certified mail, return receipt requested, and keep a copy for your records. If for some reason the credit card company is not cooperative when you call, go ahead and send the letter anyway, and send a copy to the bank's compliance officer. He or she is responsible for making sure the bank complies with federal credit laws. This will get your message across. If the matter ever goes to court, you will have a paper trail that will serve as evidence that you're not responsible for any credit card debt incurred by your separated (or ex-) spouse subsequent to your request that the account be closed.

I am married but about to get separated. Will I be responsible for any debts that my soon-to-be ex-husband accumulates after we are separated?

In most cases, you will not be responsible for the debt that a spouse incurs after the legal separation date, unless it is determined that the debt was incurred to pay for the necessities of life for the family or for the children's education.

How about the debts that my soon-to-be ex-husband incurred before we got married? Am I responsible for those?
No, not usually.

My wife and I recently got a divorce, but she continues to use our joint credit card to make purchases. Am I responsible for paying those bills?
Unfortunately, yes—unless you have notified the credit card company that you want to close the account.

My aunt has offered to help me get out of credit card debt by lending me $15,000 at a very low rate. What do you think?
Borrowing money from your aunt, or from any relative or friend, may seem like a good idea, but be prepared for the possibility that the arrangement may backfire. First, ask yourself whether the loan will really help you resolve to avoid the pitfalls of overspending—that is, to get and *stay* out of debt. In my experience, emergency bailouts often just reset the clock for people who are prone to debt.

If you do decide to borrow this money, keep things businesslike. It's only fair that you pay an interest rate above what your aunt could earn in a savings account or a money-market fund. Make the total amount of debt that you are carrying very clear to her and, if possible, sign a promissory note that spells out the terms of the loan. Otherwise, it can be too tempting not to take your aunt's loan seriously, and too easy to take on new debt. And that could mean putting your relationship with your aunt at risk.

When my parents die and their estate is settled, will I be responsible for any credit card debt they have?

You won't be personally responsible unless your name is on the account. If there is enough money in your parents' estate to pay the debt, the estate will be responsible for payment; if there is no money, most credit card companies will write off the debt owed by the deceased. (For more on estate planning and debt, please see *Ask Suze...About Wills and Trusts*.)

My husband died recently, and I am wondering how his death will affect my credit card accounts.

This is one reason I advise couples to have both joint and individual credit card accounts. If only one partner works and that partner dies, the stay-at-home partner can have trouble obtaining a card in his or her own name without a steady source of income to support the credit card application. Please do not wait until you find yourself in this situation. As for the particular situation described above, I would say that if your accounts were held jointly and you are sure you can maintain them on your own, then go ahead and tell the issuers that the accounts will now be in your name only. Also, inform the three credit bureaus that your husband has died. Otherwise you may find that other credit card companies continue to solicit him by mail.

CREDIT CARDS AND CHILDREN

I have two children, ages 10 and 13. What's the best way for me to start educating them about credit cards and debt in general?

It's never too soon to begin your children's financial education. First, be conscious of the messages you send them as you pull out your Visa card to pay for gas or meals at a favorite restaurant. Because no money changes hands, they may assume the gas or the meal is free! Explain how credit works— that the credit card company is temporarily allowing you to use its money, which is normally paid back at the end of the month. Also explain that after the end of the month the company starts charging interest, and will keep charging interest until the bill is paid in full. This is how people get into trouble.

My son, a college sophomore, has gotten himself into a fix with credit cards and owes money to the tune of nearly $3,000. I'm floored, especially since he's on financial aid! How can credit card companies let a 20-year-old spend money he doesn't have?

Your son may not be an entirely innocent victim, but the truth is, credit card companies make it fairly easy for college students to get in over their heads. Why do they target young adults? The companies know that if they can get a customer early, the customer is likely to remain loyal to—or dependent on—their product for a very long time. Often, college students don't need to show an income, or even have their application cosigned by a parent or other responsible adult, to get a credit card sent to them. Card companies assume that if college students get into trouble, their parents will bail them out—even if, legally, they don't have to.

Is it a good or a bad idea for a college student to have a credit card?

Despite the potential pitfalls, I think it's a good idea for a college student to have one credit card. The reason: As students get older, it may become harder for them to qualify for a card and to establish credit, particularly if they take their time finding a job after college.

The card and charging privileges, however, should come with strict guidelines. The credit limit should be set at $500 or $1,000 at most. A duplicate statement should be sent directly to the parents. And I'd stay away from American Express cards—the annual fee is relatively high and there are no spending limits.

My daughter is going to college next month, and she's taking her first credit card with her. What should I tell her?

Set limits on your daughter's use of the card and on her spending. For example, tell her that the card can be used only for certain kinds of purchases (e.g., airplane tickets to travel home) or in emergencies; and make sure to define an emergency! Be clear about your position on bailing her out if she runs up a debt she cannot pay—and don't budge from that position. Explain credit ratings, and tell her that wise use of this card is the way to establish a good credit rating for herself. If she skips payments or pays bills late, her credit rating will suffer, possibly affecting her purchasing power later in life, as well as her ability to get a job or to qualify for insurance.

My daughter is in college. Am I legally responsible for her credit card bills if she can't pay them?

If your name does not appear on the credit card application, then no, you are not responsible for your daughter's bills. If you cosigned the application, then you are.

CREDIT BUREAUS/
CREDIT REPORTS

What exactly is a credit rating?
"Credit rating" is shorthand for a numbered system called a
"credit scoring system." Your score, or credit rating, tells lenders
and issuers of credit—including mortgage companies, credit card
companies, retail stores, utility companies, etc.—how prompt
and responsible you have been in paying your bills and debts.
Since the rating system is pretty much universal, it is easy for
potential lenders, landlords, and even employers to evaluate your
creditworthiness and assess whether you are a good or a bad risk
when they are considering entering into a financial arrangement
with you. The document that contains the financial information that determines your credit rating is called your credit report.

Can I get a copy of my credit report?
You have the right to receive, at your request, a free copy of your
credit report once every 12 months, from each of the nation-
wide credit bureaus—Experian, TransUnion, and Equifax. You
can make your request three ways: through their central website,
www.annualcreditreport.com; by calling 1-877-322-8228, or
complete the Annual Credit Report Request Form on the website and mail it to:

Annaul Credit Report Request Service
P.O. Box 105281
Atlanta, GA 30348-5281

You also are entitled to another free report every 12
months upon request if you certify that:

- you are unemployed and plan to seek employment within 60 days;
- you are on welfare; or
- your report is inaccurate due to fraud.

Under other circumstances, a credit bureau may charge you up to $9.50 (depending on where you live) for a copy of your report.

What is a credit bureau?

A credit bureau is a company that keeps a large database of detailed financial information from which your credit report is generated and from whom credit card companies, banks, mortgage lenders, insurers, credit unions, and others purchase that information. Credit bureaus—also known as credit repackaging agencies—make a terrific living by amassing and selling data about your financial habits, history, and current spending and borrowing practices. This information, in the form of a credit report, is available to those with a legally permissible purpose to see it. Basically, it's the credit bureaus' business to find out as much as they can about your financial history.

There are three major credit bureau companies: Experian (formerly TRW Information Systems Inc.), headquartered in Orange, California; TransUnion, based in Chicago, Illinois; and Equifax (formerly CBI/Equifax), based in Atlanta, Georgia.

Their addresses, phone numbers, and websites are as follows:

Equifax
P.O. Box 740241
Atlanta, GA 30374-0241
(800) 685-1111
(800) 997-2493 for residents of Colorado, Georgia, Maryland, Massachusetts, New Jersey, or Vermont
www.econsumer.equifax.com/universal/contactus.shtml

Experian
P.O. Box 105281
Allen, TX 75013
(888) 397-3742
www.experian.com

TransUnion Corporation
Consumer Disclosure Center
P.O. Box 2000
Chester, PA 19022
(800) 888-4213 to get your credit report
(800) 916-8800 to ask questions about your report
www.transunion.com

What's in my credit report?

A standard credit report includes your name, address, date of birth, past addresses (home and work), Social Security number, phone numbers, and the names of your spouse and/or ex-spouses, if applicable. It contains a reasonably complete and up-to-date outline of your financial history, including employment history, marriages and divorces, any liens, any bankruptcy information, and, most important, a credit history. It lists the names of your creditors—including retailers, card issuers, and other lenders. In what's known as a "trade-line," it shows when you opened each of your credit accounts, whether an account is in your name only or is a joint account, how much outstanding debt you have in each account, your credit limits and current balances, and any negative information connected with your accounts, such as a history of late payments during the previous 24 to 60 months. Did someone sue you in court and win? It'll be in your credit file. Do you owe child support? It will be in your credit file. Some people may find it frightening to know that credit bureaus are keeping such detailed information about them, but not much borrowing or lending would take place without credit reports.

How often is my credit report updated?

It is updated whenever someone requests a copy of it. When a bank or an insurance or credit card company calls the credit bureau and asks for information pertaining to your credit history, the bureau puts together all the latest information in its databases. It presents this material to the lender, often via computer, as your "report."

What criteria do creditors use in deciding whether or not to extend me credit?

A lot of creditors use three guidelines when deciding whether or not to extend you credit: character, capacity, and collateral. These are sometimes known as the Three C's of good credit.

What do they mean by "character"?

From the point of view of a credit bureau, character means that you are trustworthy as far as advancing credit is concerned—i.e., that you pay your bills on time.

What does "capacity" mean?

As used by the credit bureaus, capacity refers to your financial status and stability. For example: Do you earn enough to be able to pay interest charges consistently? Do you have an alternate source of income, such as money left to you by your family or an investment portfolio, that could be drawn on in an emergency?

What does "collateral" mean?

Collateral is the material security that a lender may need in order to advance you credit or a loan. It can be a house, a car, or stock certificates. If you default on certain kinds of loans or credit lines, your lender may take possession of your collateral.

After taking these three things into consideration, how does a credit card company decide whether to accept me or turn me down?

After evaluating the Three C's, lenders turn to credit scoring to decide whether your application—for a credit card, a home equity loan, or a mortgage—should be approved or turned down.

FICO SCORE

What exactly is a FICO score?

A FICO score is a numeric value assigned to your credit habits and history by a company called Fair Isaac Company. Every American who has ever used credit now has a FICO score, and all creditors now use them. In the last few years, this score has become one of the most important criteria for evaluating you when you apply for credit. The higher your score, the lower the interest rates you may pay on credit cards, mortgages, and car loans. Conversely, the lower your score, the higher the rates you most likely will pay. To find out what your FICO score is, log on to *www.myFICO.com*. It will cost you $15.95 to get your score.

What are the different ranges of a FICO score?

FICO scores range from 300 to 850, but they are basically divided into six ranges that correspond with the interest rates that are issued by main lenders. Those who fall below the sixth range (500–579) are in what's called the "sub lenders" category. The six ranges are what you should concentrate on. The FICO score is now also being used by employers and landlords to evaluate applications. From it, they can discern your payment history and whether you are most apt to pay rent on time, so it helps them decide if they should take a risk and hire you or rent to you. Here are the six ranges:

SCORE
760–850
700–759
660–699
620–659
580–619
500–579

To be eligible for the lowest interest rate on your credit cards as well as other loans, you need to have a FICO score that is in the top range (760–850). If you are below 660, you are (in your lender's mind) a greater financial risk.

For a mortgage, can you tell me how much of a difference it makes to be ranked one range vs. another?

Well, to give you an example, below are the interest rates, as of October 10, 2006, that you might qualify for on a 30-year fixed mortgage depending on your FICO score. Notice that there is almost a 3 percent difference from the lowest range on the chart to the highest. On a $300,000 mortgage, that could be close to $650 a month savings.

SCORE	INTEREST RATE ON 30-YEAR FIXED MORTGAGE
760–850	5.97%
700–759	6.19%
660–699	6.47%
620–659	7.28%
580–619	8.27%
500–579	9.12%

I applied for a mortgage via lendingtree.com, and they put offers out to multiple banks at once to get the best rate. I was told by my friend that this will hurt my FICO score. Is he right?

Your friends are wrong. The FICO people are smart; when they sense you are shopping around for the best deal on a major purchase, such as a home or a car, they will count all lender inquiries in a 14-day period as if they were just one inquiry. LendingTree knows this as well, and it will make all its inquiries within a day or two, to avoid multiple inquiries on your credit report. So the bottom line is that if you are using a company such as LendingTree or are rate shopping on your own, just keep the search less than 14 days and you won't have any problems.

I've heard that if I pay off any balance in full, I will still need to stop using my credit cards two months before I apply for a mortgage. Is this true?

The credit scoring people can't read your mind; they have no way of knowing that your intention is to pay off the balance in full. You want to avoid a situation in which your mortgage lender happens to check your credit score just before you pay off your bill; if it's a hefty balance—even if you intend to pay it off—it's going to affect your FICO score, and that in turn can affect whether you get a mortgage, or the rate that you will be offered.

If I have a good FICO score, how do I get the interest rates on my credit card lowered?

If your FICO score is really good (720 or above) then you should be aware that technically you qualify to get the best (that is, the lowest) interest rates available on the money you borrow. If this is the case and you are paying a high interest rate on your credit cards, call your credit card company and say that if they do not lower your interest rate, you will be switching your account. You might want to actually try to get a card with a better rate first and, when you do, make your current card company beat that rate; if it does not, transfer your credit balance to the new account. But before you close down that first account altogether, read about how closing an account could hurt a FICO score in the question below. To find the best interest rate on credit cards, log on to *www.lend ingtree.com* or *www.bankrate.com*.

I currently have a zero percent rate on my credit cards, and I keep switching to new ones. I was told that this will hurt my FICO score. Is this true?

Yes, it's true that constantly opening new credit card accounts can hurt your credit score. Creditors will think that you are gearing up for a big spending spree, and that will cause problems with your FICO score. To avoid needlessly alarming the credit folks, don't shop for new cards more than once every six months.

Will closing an account hurt my FICO score?

It depends. It is possible that it could hurt your score in two ways. The first way is in regard to your credit history, which accounts for 15 percent of your score. If you have four credit cards that you got more than ten years ago, you have a reported credit history on those cards that goes back ten years. If, however, you decide to get a new card with a better interest rate and close down all the other accounts, your reported credit history will also be closed down. This will count against you. So sometimes, especially on the older cards on which you do not pay a yearly fee, you may be better off keeping them and not using them. Closing them down and shortening your history may hurt your score.

The second way is in regard to your debt-to-credit-limit ratio, which accounts for 30 percent of your FICO score. Imagine that you have four cards, each with a credit limit of $2,000, for a total combined credit limit of $8,000. In your wisdom, you have only ever used one of those cards, which currently has a balance on it of about $1,500. Your debt-to-credit-limit ratio (how much you owe vs. how much credit you have) is about 19 percent ($1,500 divided by $8,000). If you think, "Well, I am not using my other cards, so I should just close them," be careful. If you close an account you are not using, your FICO score may be affected negatively. In the above example, if you have only one card open, which has a credit limit of $2,000, and you have a balance of $1,500, that makes your debt-to-credit-limit ratio 75 percent—bad news for your FICO score. Believe it or not, you just might be better off leaving the extra cards open and unused.

If I have a high debt-to-credit-limit ratio, is there anything I can do to improve my FICO score?

Yes. You could call and ask your credit card holders to raise your credit limits, and that would bring down your ratio. So, for instance, let's say you have five credit cards with a limit of $2,000 on each, for $10,000 of credit total. But you have used $8,000 of that credit. That gives you an 80 percent debt-to-credit-limit ratio—and that is high. Let's say you call all five credit card companies and get them to raise your credit limits on each card to $4,000. Now your credit limit is $20,000, but you still only owe $8,000, so your debt-to-credit-limit ratio is now only 40 percent. Big difference.

Are there any dangers to calling a credit card company and asking them to raise your limits?

Yes. The first is they may not want to do it. The second is that before you know it, you may have charged even more. So, in the question before, where you only owed $8,000, you now may owe $15,000 or even more. So you must be careful, for regardless of your FICO score, you do need to repay the money that you charge, so you best have the money to pay it back.

Will my score drop if I apply for new credit?

If it does, it probably won't drop much. If you apply for several credit cards within a short period of time, multiple requests for your credit report information (called "inquiries") will appear on your report. Looking for new credit can be equated with higher risk, but most credit scores are not affected by multiple inquiries from auto or mortgage lenders within a short period of time—usually two weeks. Typically, these are treated as a single inquiry and will have little impact on your credit score.

Will reducing my debt help my FICO score?

Reducing your debt figures largely in your FICO score. You do yourself a huge favor by eliminating all credit card debt, or at least by not using your cards as often. The goal here is to improve your credit score, and one way of doing that is to widen the gap between what you owe and what your credit limit is. The less you owe, the better your FICO score becomes.

Will paying cash for purchases help my FICO score?

Your FICO score goes up when the credit bureaus see your balances going down. Especially in the months before you apply for a loan, be very careful how much debt you are putting on your cards. If you need to buy something, buy it in cash, if possible. Pay cash when you eat out, go to the movies, shop for groceries, or buy clothes. If you do not have the money to pay cash for something at this point, just don't buy it! Charging all those things could hurt your FICO score.

Will paying my bills late affect my FICO score?

Paying your bills by the due date accounts for 35 percent of your FICO score, so this is extremely important for your current payment history. Do everything you can to get your payments in on time, no matter what, especially in the months prior to applying for a loan. A late or missed payment close to the time that you apply for a loan will lower your score far more than an isolated late payment some years in the past. It can seriously hurt your score, sometimes to the tune of about 75 points. That one skipped payment could take you from a good rating to a horrible one.

Will using a credit counseling service hurt my FICO score?

In years past, using a credit counseling service actually hurt your FICO score, but this is not as true today. The wise people at FICO have realized that people who use a credit counselor want to help themselves and are not trying to avoid paying their bills, so they do not mark down your score as they used to. If you doubt that you can tackle your credit card debt on your own, and you feel that you need help, contact a credit counseling service, such as the National Foundation for Credit Counseling (*www.nfcc.org* or (800) 388-2227). These people are experienced, helpful, and relatively inexpensive to use (in 2006, the average cost for a budget counseling session was $25; the average Debt Management Plan [DMP] enrollment fee was $50; and the average fee for monthly DMP services was around $25 total). They may even be able to negotiate a lower rate or a repayment schedule for you.

What will declaring bankruptcy do to my FICO score?

If you declare bankruptcy, you won't be able to do much to get your score up for a number of years. Bankruptcies stay on your credit report for ten years, and they are an immediate markdown of at least 200 points, even if you had a good credit score prior to the bankruptcy. Just because you have claimed bankruptcy, however, does not mean that you cannot get credit. In many cases, there are lenders who will be all over you like a cheap suit. They know that, legally, you cannot claim bankruptcy again for at least six years. So during those years, they just love to sock it to you with interest rates that are sky-high. Be careful. A number of people who claim bankruptcy have to claim it twice. Your FICO score aside, in my opinion, bankruptcy is a very serious action to take; you need to seek the best advice and think about it carefully. It may or may not make sense for you in your particular situation.

Does using a debit card or prepaid credit card affect my FICO score?

No. Debit cards or prepaid cards do not build your FICO score. But secured credit cards—cards that are secured against your savings account—which are often an option for people with bad or no credit, do count toward building your FICO score.

How can my children build credit and their FICO scores when they're in college, without getting their own credit cards?

If Mom and Dad add their child as an authorized user on one of their credit cards, it is easy for their child to begin building a credit record, and thus a FICO score. Parents should choose the card that has the longest history, the best payment record, and the highest limit. Once the child is added to that card (regardless of whether Mom and Dad actually give them the card and let them use it), that "tradeline" gets added to the child's credit report, and the FICO score thinks it's the child's account (as well as Mom and Dad's). If for some reason Mom and Dad don't keep up with payments, the child can choose to have his or her name deleted from the account; there will be no lasting negative impact on the child's FICO score because Mom and Dad didn't pay their bills.

How can I improve my FICO score?

It's important to note that raising your score is a bit like losing weight: It takes time and there is no quick fix. In fact, quick-fix efforts can backfire. The best advice is to manage your credit responsibility over time. Generally, people with high FICO scores consistently pay bills on time, keep balances low on credit cards and other revolving credit products, and apply for and open new credit accounts only as needed. Below are tips on how to improve your FICO score. You can also go to *www.myFICO.com* to use a simulator that will show you how to improve your score in your particular situation.

- *Pay your bills on time.* Delinquent payments and collections can have a major negative impact on your score. If you have missed payments, get current and stay current. The longer you pay your bills on time, the better your score will be.
- *If you are having trouble making ends meet, contact your creditors or see a legitimate credit counselor.* This won't improve your score immediately, but if you can begin to manage your credit and pay bills on time, your score will get better in time.
- *Keep balances low.* High outstanding debt—on credit cards, lines of credit, and other "revolving credit"—can adversely affect a score.
- *Pay off debt rather than moving it around.* The most effective way to improve your score in this area is by paying down your revolving credit. In fact, owing

the same amount but having fewer open accounts may lower your score.

- **_Don't close unused credit cards as a short-term strategy to raise your score._** When you close unused credit cards, it lowers the amount of credit available to you without changing the amount of your debt. On paper, you appear to be closer to maxing out your credit cards, so closing unused credit cards could backfire and actually lower your score.

- **_Don't open a number of new credit cards that you don't need just to increase your available credit._** FICO scores always take into account the following: how many new accounts you have, how long it has been since you opened a new account, how many recent requests for credit you have made, as indicated by inquiries to the credit reporting agencies, and the length of time since credit report inquiries were made by lenders. When you open new credit cards that you don't need, you can hurt all the factors listed above. That effect can outweigh any beneficial action of increasing your available credit and can result in a lower FICO score.

- **_If you have been managing credit for a short time, don't open a lot of new accounts too rapidly._** New accounts will lower your average account age, which will have a larger effect on your score if you don't have a lot of other credit information. Also, rapid account buildup can look risky if you are a new credit user.

- **_Do your rate shopping for a given loan within a focused period of time._** FICO scores distinguish between a search for a single loan and a search for many new credit lines, in part by the length of time over which inquiries occur. So don't window-shop for a loan over time; focus on what you need, get the best deal you can, and make a decision.

- **Reestablish your credit history if you have had problems.** Opening new accounts responsibly and paying them off on time will raise your score in the long term.
- **Have credit cards—but manage them responsibly.** In general, having credit cards and installment loans (and making timely payments) will raise your score. Someone with no credit cards, for example, tends to be a higher risk than someone who has managed credit cards responsibly.
- **Note that it's OK to request and check your own credit report.** This won't affect your score, as long as you order your credit report directly from the credit reporting agency or through an organization authorized to provide credit reports to consumers.
- **Note that closing an account doesn't make it go away.** A closed account will still show up on your credit report, and it may affect your score.

How often does my score change?

Because your FICO score is calculated anew every time a lender or potential lender asks to see it, your score today is likely different from your score of just a few weeks ago. The score is calculated based on the latest snapshot of information contained in your credit report at the time the score is requested. In general, your score changes when the underlying information on your credit report changes. Fluctuations of a few points from month to month are common.

I have become obsessed with checking my FICO score. Does it count against me if I check it all the time?

There's no problem if *you* are checking your score. The only problems arise when potential lenders are constantly checking your score; that's a sign that you may be trying to take on too much credit or debt. But even though you can check to your heart's delight without triggering any red flags, I don't think that's a particularly good use of your time. It's important to realize that it can take months for your credit information to be updated and to be reflected in your FICO score, so constant monitoring isn't going to get you anywhere.

How much will my score change over time?
How much your score changes depends on how you are managing your credit. If you manage your credit consistently over time, your score should remain quite stable. You'll see bigger changes in your score if you significantly change your credit behavior by opening new credit accounts, for example, or if you change account balances in a big way, or don't pay your bills on time. In general, it is a good idea to check your score at least once a year. If you are working to improve your score, you may want to check it every quarter or even every month.

If I've been denied credit, will the credit bureau tell me why?
You are entitled to receive a free copy of your credit report from the bureau that supplied the information to your prospective lender, and it will tell you exactly why you were denied. You must ask for a copy within 60 days of being denied credit. In general, I recommend that you check your credit status from time to time, in order to make sure that it is completely accurate.

What should I look for when I receive my credit report?
You should check everything for accuracy. Make a list of items that are incorrect, out-of-date, or misleading. In particular,

look for mistakes in your name, address, phone number, or Social Security number, and for missing or outdated employment information. Your credit report also will list the names of people or companies that have requested your file within the last six months (or two years, if the information was requested by an employer or a potential employer), which will give you useful information.

What shouldn't be in my credit report?

Be on the lookout for bankruptcies that are more than ten years old, any negative information about you that is more than seven years old, credit inquiries older than two years, credit accounts that are not yours, incorrect account histories (especially late payments when you've paid on time), a missing notation when you've disputed a charge on a credit card bill, closed accounts incorrectly listed as open, and any account that is not listed as "closed by consumer," because if your report doesn't note this, the account will appear to have been closed by the creditor in question.

What rights do I have with credit bureaus?

Recent laws oblige credit bureaus to establish toll-free numbers so that if you have a question or a problem, you can contact them without charge. The law also specifies that the bureaus provide a human service representative rather than a computer voice on the other end of the line.

What should I do if I find something listed incorrectly on my credit report?

If you find mistakes on your credit report, fill out the "Request for Reinvestigation" form that accompanies the report. If you did not receive this form, write to the credit bureau and ask for one. List on the form each incorrect item and explain exactly what is wrong. Be sure to make a copy of the form before sending it back. The reinvestigation is free.

Does the credit bureau have to remove inaccurate information from my credit report?

Yes. If something in your credit report is incorrect, or if the creditor who provided the information can no longer verify it, the credit bureau must remove the information from your file. Often, credit bureaus will remove information without reinvestigating it if reinvestigation is more bother than it is worth.

If the bureau reinvestigates, how long will that take?

Once the credit bureau receives your reinvestigation request, it must get back to you within a "reasonable" time. By law, that usually means 30 days, although many bureaus will respond within ten days. Reinvestigation is an easy process for the bureaus, since computers link them all.

If you have found errors in a report issued by one bureau— and don't be surprised if you do—you might want to play it safe and obtain copies of your report from the two other major bureaus, check them thoroughly, and ask that any errors appearing in them be corrected.

What happens if the credit bureau doesn't respond?

If you don't hear from the credit bureau within 30 days, send a follow-up letter. Make it clear that you are sending a copy of your second letter to the Federal Trade Commission at 600 Pennsylvania Avenue NW, Washington, DC 20580. That will really grab the bureau's attention.

My credit bureau seems to be stonewalling me. Do I have any recourse?

If you feel the credit bureau is not abiding by the law or has treated you unfairly, you can send a complaint directly to the Federal Trade Commission. Be sure to send along a copy of all your correspondence with the credit bureau. If a credit bureau insists on reporting out-of-date or inaccurate information, writing to the FTC can put an end to it.

Can I add things to my report that I feel are worth mentioning?

Absolutely. If you feel the need to explain a particular entry, you are entitled to add a 100-word statement to your file. Because the credit bureau is required to set down only a summary of what you write, be extremely concise and clear. You can also add positive items to your file—for example, accounts that you've paid on time. Just ask in writing that the information be added to your report.

DENIED CREDIT

I have good credit, but while searching for a better interest rate, I applied for five low-interest-rate credit cards. I was turned down by all of them. Why?

Probably because the flurry of activity showed up on your credit report. Such activity makes lenders wary. They assume you are about to go on a spending spree and possibly put yourself into big-time debt. Did it ever occur to them that you might be comparison shopping for a credit card? Of course not. My advice to you now is to wait at least six months before applying for a new credit card. While you wait, check the rates on several cards and select one—and only one—to apply for. (Log on to *www.bankrate.com* for current cards and rates.) And take advantage of the fact that getting turned down means you can request for free another copy of your credit report, in addition to the free report you're entitled to yearly from the national credit bureaus.

I was just denied a credit card, and one of the reasons the company cited was age. I am 35 years old. What's going on here? Is this legal?

A credit card company can legally take age into consideration when it assesses the application of anyone between 18 and 61 years old. As part of the screening process, companies compare your financial data with that of other people your age. If your profile comes up short compared to other 35-year-olds, you will pay the price.

My aunt, who is 75, recently applied for her first credit card and had a lot of trouble getting one. I would think that elderly people would be the best credit risks of all!

Not as far as the credit card companies are concerned. Companies are required, however, not to discriminate against older people solely on the basis of age, so if your aunt has a good financial record, she should get the credit she needs. In a landmark 1988 case, the Federal Trade Commission charged in court that a certain finance company was breaking credit protection laws by extending loans to older applicants on far less favorable terms than to younger applicants. It won the case, citing the 1975 Equal Credit Opportunity Act (ECOA), which made it illegal for a creditor to turn down an applicant just because he or she is 62 years old or older. The ECOA requires creditors to figure in income other than wages, such as pensions and annuities, when estimating the financial resources of older citizens—very important, since many older people are retired and no longer earn a salary. It also prevents creditors from changing the terms of a loan or adding interest simply because a person is approaching retirement age. Your aunt should register a complaint with the FTC against the companies that gave her a hard time.

BAD CREDIT RATINGS

Millions of Americans have bad credit ratings, often signaled by FICO scores below about 660. (For more about FICO scores and how to improve them, see page 50.) A bad rating doesn't necessarily mean that you're a deadbeat or a slacker. In today's economic turmoil it may mean that you have run into financial difficulties due to a loss of job, divorce, or illness situations that set many people back temporarily. Millions of Americans have managed to repair their credit ratings, and chances are that you can, too.

I've been told I have a bad credit rating. How did that come about?

A lot of factors—or maybe just one—can contribute to a bad credit rating. Yours could have been caused by a history of late payments on your mortgage, utilities, car, or credit cards. Or perhaps a credit card company forgave your having been a few days late in paying a large balance you owed, but got annoyed when your balance of $13 took you nearly four months to repay and reported you to the credit bureau. There may be a notation in your credit file to the effect that you have not honored certain debts to the IRS, or that you have not paid out a lawsuit you lost, or that you've fallen behind on child-support payments. Or your bad credit rating could have been caused by something much larger and more serious, like a bankruptcy, which is considered the worst indicator of creditworthiness on a credit report.

What are the warning signs of a so-so or a bad credit report?

Most people who have a bad credit report are well aware of the fact—that is, if they are being honest with themselves. They start to notice a pattern. Creditors begin calling to find out what happened to the payment that was due three months ago. They have a history of getting notices from collection services. When they apply for a new credit card, they get turned down. But there's only one sure way to find out if you have a bad credit report—and that is by requesting a copy from one of the big three credit bureaus, along with a copy of your current FICO score. (For information on how to contact the credit bureaus, see page 47.)

How long will negative information stay on my credit report?

Negative information typically remains on your credit report for seven years. This includes late payments, paid and unpaid lawsuits and judgments, paid and unpaid tax liens, collection-agency or profit-and-loss accounts (an account that a lender has written off as not worth pursuing but that nevertheless goes on your credit report), and records of arrest, indictment, or conviction of a crime. If you declare Chapter 7 bankruptcy, this information will appear on your credit reports for ten years—but no longer. All three of the major credit bureaus will remove successfully completed Chapter 13 bankruptcies (this is the kind where you have paid back a portion of your debts) seven years from the filing date.

How does a bad credit rating affect a person's day-to-day financial life?

A bad credit rating can make getting a credit card difficult—and if you can't get a credit card, there are a lot of other things you can't do. You will run into trouble renting a car, making an airplane reservation, even renting a video. If you don't have a credit card, you may be asked to put down a sizable amount of money as a deposit for everything from a special-order book to such essentials as heat and electricity.

I know I have a problem with my credit rating. What can I do to fix it?

Along with taking steps to improve your FICO score (see page 58), here are some tips to begin to generate a good new credit history for yourself:

- Apply for credit with a local retailer, such as a department store.
- Make a large down payment on a purchase and negotiate credit payments for the balance.
- Apply for a small loan at a bank or credit union where you have checking and savings accounts.

If you are rejected for credit in any of these venues, find out why. You may have been denied credit for not meeting the creditor's minimum income requirement or not having been at your address or job for the required length of time. You can overcome these obstacles with time.

If you are still unable to get credit, you may wish to ask a friend or relative with an established credit history to act as a cosigner. A cosigner promises to repay the debt if you don't. An account established with a cosigner will usually be reported on both your own and your cosigner's credit reports.

Once you have obtained credit, pay your bills consistently and on time. By doing so, you establish a positive credit history that helps you obtain future credit for larger purchases, such as a house or car.

I was recently laid off from work and was late on a credit card payment. A friend told me I should request

a goodwill adjustment. Can you tell me more about this?

If you have run into a situation, such as an illness or a job loss, that causes you to be late making a payment, a goodwill adjustment is an option you can consider to avoid having the late payment appear on your credit report and hurt your FICO score. You need to contact the creditor, explain your situation, and request that your account be "re-aged." If your account is re-aged, it will be reported as current rather than late. This procedure is called goodwill adjustment because the creditor does it to help the customer get back on his or her feet. Please be aware that requesting a goodwill adjustment can be time-consuming, since you may need to make several calls and in most cases will need to speak to a manager or supervisor in order to get the adjustment. Now, just because you request an adjustment does not mean it is automatic; it's at your creditor's discretion whether they choose to honor your request. Some creditors choose not to offer goodwill adjustments, in part because late fees generate a significant amount of revenue. Also, federal guidelines only permit creditors or banks to re-age an account once every 12 months and twice every five years. Creditors may also require two or more consecutive monthly payments to be on time before they will make a goodwill adjustment. But it is definitely worth it to ask that your account be re-aged, since a late payment on your credit report can hurt your FICO score. Make sure you also request a copy of all paperwork that the creditor sends to the credit bureaus, just in case the goodwill adjustment is not properly reported and you need to correct your credit report at a later date.

TAKING CONTROL OF
YOUR CREDIT CARD DEBT

If I realize that my debt is spiraling out of control, should I cut up my credit cards?

Absolutely. Take a pair of scissors and cut up each and every credit card in your wallet, but do not cancel your credit cards—it can hurt your new FICO score (see page 53). Remember to follow up with a letter, keeping a copy for your records as well. Putting a stop to the vicious cycle of using credit cards to cover cash shortfalls caused by previous debt or continuing to spend more than you have in the bank is a first, crucial step in taking control of your debt.

I'm scared not to have at least one credit card to carry with me. What about emergencies?

If you feel this way, cut up all your credit cards but one, and carry this card in case of emergencies. You can safeguard against overspending with this card by calling the credit card company and asking to have your credit limit lowered to an amount you might need in an emergency—say, $500 or $1,000.

OK, I've cut up my credit cards. How do I begin to deal with what I owe?

Good! Now, this step may seem difficult, because it asks you to sit down, study your statements, face what you owe, and see what the credit card companies are charging you to owe it. It's the "honesty" step. Here's what to do. Make a list of all the amounts of money you owe, starting not with the largest amount but with the balance on which you pay the highest interest rate. Then list your balances in descending order, by interest rate. Include all your creditors—and I mean *everybody*, from Visa to your sister. Don't forget to include student loans, any money you owe the IRS, and personal debts. About the last item, remember: Debt is debt, and just because most personal debt doesn't inspire the same fear as credit card debt doesn't mean it isn't weighing, pound for pound, on your self-respect. List the amount you owe, the interest rate, the minimum monthly payment, and how your creditor charges you interest (average daily or two-cycle average daily). Also list your creditors' phone numbers. For an example, see the table below.

I owe late payments to some of my creditors. What should I do?

This is where the phone numbers come in. If you're late in making a payment on any of your debts, personal or institutional, call up the person or institution you've borrowed money from right now. Explain why your payment is late. Your

SAMPLE LIST OF CREDIT CARD BALANCES, HIGHEST INTEREST RATE FIRST

CREDITOR	BALANCE OWED	INTEREST RATE	PAYMENT	CYCLE	PHONE NUMBER
Department store	$4,320	21%	$180	Average daily	_____
Visa	$6,300	18.9%	$200	2-cycle average daily	_____
Department store	$3,100	16.9%	$100	2-cycle average daily	_____
Optima	$4,000	7.9%	$120	Average daily	_____
Mom	$5,000	0	0	0	_____

creditors already know you don't have the money to pay the bill or else you would have, so don't be embarrassed. If the person on the other end of the line is rude to you, be gracious. If you will have the money in two weeks, or can send only $25, say so. In any case, it's important that you call your creditors before they call you.

Until I made my list, I wasn't fully aware of the astronomical interest rates I'm paying. Can I have them lowered?

Yes, especially if you have a good FICO score (see page 50). If you have a regular, punctual payment history, it's a very good idea to call and ask to have your interest rates lowered on outstanding debt. First, take a look at what some lower-interest-rate cards are charging. Then call your highest-interest-rate credit card companies, tell them you're considering switching to a better value card, and see if they'll match a lower rate. You can negotiate with them, and often they will reduce your interest rate right on the spot. If they won't, simply move your balance to a card that offers a lower rate. Make sure you cancel the first card after you've transferred your balance.

If you have a low FICO score or history of late payments or other problems with your credit report, you may not be able to negotiate a better rate or switch to a lower-rate card.

I'm looking at the list of what I owe, and it makes me sick. How will I ever get out of this mess?

You can and will get out of debt, a step—and a month—at a time. After you've negotiated the lowest interest rates you can, the single most effective action you can take is to begin paying more than the minimum amounts due each month. On the next page is a plan to follow.

YOUR CREDIT CARD DEBT

- First step: Figure out the largest possible amount you can afford to pay each month toward all your credit card balances together. Let's say that amount is $300 a month. You may think this is a lot, but when you carry a lot of debt on at least several different cards, this amount is probably close to what you already pay when the minimum payments are added together.
- Second step: Add $10 to each minimum payment that your credit card company is asking you to pay.
- Third step: Add up all your minimum payments plus the $10 you added for each card. Let's say the minimum payment plus $10 for all your cards together is $200. You've decided that you can pay a total of $300 a month toward eradicating your debt. Subtract the $200 you must pay from the $300 you can pay, and this leaves you with an additional $100 to pay on your credit card debt.
- Making payments: Now you are going to take the "extra" $100 a month and put it toward the credit card that is charging you the highest interest rate. When that card is paid off, call the company and close the account for good.
- Ongoing plan: Now start all over. Let's say you were paying $130 a month on the high-interest credit card account that has now been paid off and closed. Stick with paying a total of $300 a month—unless you can raise it! Factor in all the minimum payments on your remaining cards, plus the $10 additional payment that you are making on each card. Let's say that the total monthly tab now equals $170. Apply the $130 you were paying on the closed account to the card that is *now* charging you the highest interest rate. When this card is paid off, call the company and cancel that card. Then start all over again with the third-highest-rate card.

This process may take months or even years to complete, but if you keep paying more than the minimum amount you owe each month, the strategy will work every time. Keep transferring accounts for the best interest rate deals whenever you can, and be sure to track your payments and your monthly statements carefully. Take pleasure and pride in watching the amount you owe become smaller. With each payment, you will be closer to being debt-free.

Why is paying more than the minimum monthly balance so important?

The answer is in the numbers. Let's say you owe $1,100 on a credit card that charges you 18.5 percent interest. If you pay the minimum (let's say it's 1.7 percent) of your balance every month and you never charge another item, it will take you 12 years and six months to pay off your debt. That's a very long time! And your $1,100 balance will have cost you about $1,400 in interest. If, however, you had paid $10 more than the minimum each month, you would have reduced your payment period to six years and cut your total interest payments to $676.37. Ten dollars a month is only 35 cents a day, but it adds up to a savings of about $700 in interest.

Which is more important, increasing my monthly payment or getting a lower interest rate on my balance?

Both are extremely important. With most credit cards, the more you owe and the higher the interest rate, the longer it takes you to pay everything off. This is compounded interest working against you. In some cases, if you owed $4,000 or more, had an 18 percent interest rate, and paid just the minimum every month, it would take you 40 years to pay off the debt, to say nothing of the thousands and thousands in interest it would cost you.

On the next page is a chart that will show you, pretty conclusively, what a difference a little more money each month *and* a lower interest rate can really make.

Where do I find the money to pay more than the minimum required?

Here's how you do it. From this point on, I want you to spend only paper money. If you go into a store and buy something for $4.25, and give the cashier a $5 bill, take the $0.75 change and put it into your pocket. If you go into another store and buy a pack of gum, do not take the $0.75 out of your pocket. Use a dollar bill to pay for the gum. Take that change and put it into your pocket. At the end of the day, put your accumulated change into a special jar or cup. If you spend only paper money from this point on and save your change, you will have about $30 to $60 worth of change at the end of every month to put toward your credit card debt.

I owe $8,000 in credit card debt, and I have $8,000 in my money-market fund. Should I take the money out of my money-market fund to pay off my credit card?

In truth, if you have $8,000 of credit card debt at a 14 percent annual interest rate (which is the current national average) and you are keeping $8,000 in a money-market fund on which you are earning 5 percent a year (5 percent that is *taxable* to you), you are losing more than 9 percent a year on your money for that false sense of security. This makes no sense at all. You are saving money, but it may be costing you your financial future.

Since you have the money to pay off your credit cards, here's what I want you to do. Pay off the cards. Once you've done that, take the entire payment you had been making on your cards each month (that is, when you were paying the minimum amount due, or slightly more) and put that exact

THE IMPORTANCE OF GETTING
A LOWER INTEREST RATE
LOAN AMOUNT: $4,000

ANNUAL PERCENTAGE RATE	MONTHLY PAYMENT	AMOUNT OF TIME REQUIRED TO PAY OFF DEBT	TOTAL INTEREST PAID
5.9	$100	45 months	$465
5.9	$110	40 months	$417
5.9	$150	29 months	$298
5.9	$200	22 months	$221
7.9	$100	47 months	$658
7.9	$110	42 months	$587
7.9	$150	30 months	$413
7.9	$200	22 months	$303
9.9	$100	49 months	$874
9.9	$110	44 months	$775
9.9	$150	31 months	$536
9.9	$200	21 months	$389
12.9	$100	53 months	$1,257
12.9	$110	47 months	$1,101
12.9	$150	32 months	$739
12.9	$200	23 months	$528
15.9	$100	58 months	$1,736
15.9	$110	50 months	$1,494
15.9	$150	34 months	$968
15.9	$200	24 months	$678
18.9	$100	63 months	$2,362
18.9	$110	54 months	$1,986
18.9	$150	35 months	$1,229
18.9	$200	25 months	$842

amount back into your money-market fund each month. Within a relatively short period of time, you'll have your savings back—and more. At the same time, you must stop charging things you don't need. Try to pay cash for any purchases you make, so you don't add to your debt.

Meanwhile, if an unforeseen crisis happens and you do need extra money before your nest egg is back to its former size, you can take out a cash advance on your now pristine credit card account or on an equity line of credit. You may have noticed that the interest rate on a cash advance is higher than what you are currently paying on your credit cards. Even if it is slightly higher than the national average on credit cards—it's about 18 percent these days for cash advances, 4 points higher than the credit card rate—you can always transfer your balance (even if it is made up of a cash advance) from that credit card to a new credit card at a lower introductory interest rate if your credit rating is good.

My credit card company tells me that I can eliminate my entire debt by paying 50 percent of what I owe. I owe $3,000. Is this a good idea?

The credit card company is trying to cut its losses by offering you a settlement. This may seem like an easy way out, but if you accept the settlement offer, it could affect your ability to get credit in the future.

Why? If you pay 50 percent of your outstanding balance, or $1,500, your credit report will note that the account is now "settled in full." But the credit report also will show a balance remaining on the account—the $1,500 you did not pay—as well as a note explaining this settlement. This flag will remain on your credit report for seven years. Is it worth it? Only you can decide.

Can I negotiate with credit card companies?

Yes. If you have any accounts that are currently in trouble because your payments have been late or incomplete, you are, strangely enough, in a fairly good bargaining position. Offer the credit company, or even the collection agency, full or partial payment in exchange for its agreement to remove any negative information about your account from your credit report. Some creditors and collection agencies may be willing to do this, though others may not like this idea in the slightest—you'll never know until you try.

CREDIT COUNSELING

What is a credit counseling service?

Reputable and consumer-oriented credit counseling services are typically nonprofit agencies that help consumers who are having trouble with debt. For a fee, a counselor will sit down with you and discuss all the elements of your debt, review all of your options, and help you figure out the best way to get out of debt. Sometimes he or she will even negotiate on your behalf, establish a debt management plan, and advise you of the possible consequences of declaring bankruptcy.

Are all credit counseling services the same?

Please be very careful selecting a counseling service, because all credit counselors are not the same. The credit counseling industry today has become increasingly competitive due to credit card debt now topping $800 billion in the United States, with nearly nine million people contacting a consumer credit counseling agency each year. A recent report released by the National Consumer Law Center and the Consumer Federation of America, titled *Credit Counseling in Crisis,* found the honest, reputable agencies are losing out to companies that are in the nonprofit credit counseling business to make quick money. Instead of offering a range of diagnostic and counseling services, these companies sell debt consolidation as a solution for nearly every person with debt problems. Some of the less reputable credit counseling agencies often harm rather than help, with improper advice, deceptive practices, excessive fees, and abuse of their non-profit status. That being said, if you find you need help, one of the best credit counseling services, in my opinion, is the National Foundation for Credit Counseling *(www.nfcc.org),* at (800) 388-2227. These people are experienced, helpful, and relatively inexpensive to use (in 2006, the average cost for a budget counseling session was $25; the average Debt Management Plan [DMP] enrollment fee was $50; and the average fee for monthly DMP services was around $25 total). They may even be able to negotiate a lower rate or a repayment schedule for you.

What is a debt-management plan?
A debt-management plan, or DMP, is a voluntary arrangement between you, your creditors, and the Consumer Credit Counseling Service. A DMP does two things at once: It helps you get out of debt in an honorable, organized way, and it helps your creditors get back the money you owe them. Here's how it works: A consumer agrees to deposit a certain amount of money each month in an account and the counseling service distributes this money among the consumer's creditors. Incidentally, if you enter into a DMP, many creditors will agree to lower their interest rates and fees or, in some cases, eliminate them altogether. Your credit counselor can fill you in on the details of your credit card companies' policies.

What is the impact of a debt-management plan on a FICO score?
The company whose credit score model is widely used in the

credit industry, Fair Isaac Company (FICO), has publicly stated that since 1999, FICO has completely ignored any credit report mention of credit counseling, debt-management plans, or any other form of counseling. So using a credit counseling service does not hurt your FICO score.

As for a consumer's ability to obtain credit, it is at the discretion of individual creditors how they interpret a consumer's credit report history and whether or not they will extend credit. Many creditors see a debt-management plan as a positive step and will recognize that consumers are making an effort to regain control of their finances, to reverse a negative payment history, and to avoid writing off an account or bankruptcy. While the initial impact of a debt-management plan may be minimal, there is direct positive impact over time that helps a consumer's credit standing. After a client has made numerous timely payments through a debt-management plan, some creditors will remove any references of a debt-management plan arrangement from a client's credit report. The client's credit report will reflect that they are meeting their debt obligations, which improves a client's score over time.

What questions should I ask a credit counseling service?

It is important to first learn about what credit counselors can and cannot do for you. The best way to do this is to list all your debts and categorize them as secured or unsecured. Credit counselors cannot help you with secured debt, such as your home or car loan. If you decide you want to get help from a credit counselor:

1. Ask for information about the agency before signing up. You do not need to provide personal information in order to find out the basics of what an agency can do for you.

2. Ask about counselor qualifications. How are the counselors trained?

3. Ask about privacy. Does the agency protect consumer information? Do they sell consumer information to others?

4. Ask about both DMP and non-DMP services. A DMP is not likely to work for you if you are most concerned about secured debts, such as home or car loans. But you may benefit from non-DMP counseling and/or diagnostic services.

5. If a DMP is not right for you, ask about the other services the agency provides. Be very cautious if the agency says that they only do debt consolidation or debt-management plans.

6. If you are interested in a DMP, ask how the plans work. What sorts of concessions are likely? Will the agency help with all your unsecured debts? Can you get regular account information? How often are payments made? How long is it likely to take to complete the plan?

7. Ask about any educational courses or seminars the agency provides.

8. Be sure to ask about fees. If the agency tells you a fee is voluntary, get specifics on what that means. Find out how much you will be paying an agency. If the agency is reluctant to talk about fees, you should look elsewhere.

9. Ask how working with a credit counselor will affect your credit rating.

10. Be sure credit counseling is the right solution for you before you sign up. You should also understand the alternatives to counseling, such as negotiating on your own and/or declaring bankruptcy.

I went to a credit counseling company, and they said they would charge me $800 up front and that I should stop paying my credit card bills altogether. They told me that with their help, this would lead to a deduction in what I owe. Is this true?

Please steer clear of this company. This is how unscrupulous services typically work—they ask for money up front, plus a percentage of what they claim to save you. And they really make a mess of things; in negotiating a lower payment with your creditors, they typically ruin your credit record. Here's how: They tell the creditors you do not have a penny to your name. They offer your creditor two options: accept a super-low payment or accept zippo. The creditor might accept the lower payment—rather than get nothing—but they are not going to be happy about this. So they will report to the credit bureaus that you are a terrible credit risk. That's going to make it difficult for you to ever get a decent deal on a loan or credit card in the future. It's better to work with a reputable non-profit credit counseling company such as NFCC or to contact the creditor directly and try to work out a plan in which you agree to pay a certain amount each month. The creditors want to get their money back, so they are going to try to work out a deal with you.

CREDIT REPAIR CLINICS

What about the credit repair clinics, or "credit doctors," that are advertised in newspapers and the mail, and on radio, television, and the Internet, that promise that negative information can be removed from your credit file for a fee?

Credit repair clinics should be avoided at all costs. They can't do anything for you that you can't do for yourself. No one can instantly repair credit. Only time, deliberate effort, and a personal debt-repayment plan will improve your credit. Credit protection and credit repair scams are some of the top consumer complaints reported to the FTC; the FTC estimates the loss to consumers is easily in the millions. Please be very careful if they ask you to make false statements on a loan or credit application, misrepresent your Social Security number, or advise you to get an Employer Identification Number from the Internal Revenue Service under false pretenses—you will be committing fraud. The truth is that you can help *yourself* rebuild a better credit record. Start by contacting your creditors when you realize that you are unable to make payments. If you need help working out a payment plan and a budget, contact your local credit counseling services, such as NFCC. NFCC services are available at little cost. Also, check with your employer, credit union, or housing authority for no-cost credit counseling programs.

What do credit repair clinics do that is so bad?
One thing credit repair clinics do is appeal to your paranoid side. The world of finance and of big government is not on your side, they claim, and with their enormous knowledge of various "loopholes," they can help get you out of debt. What they are usually doing is paraphrasing the portion of the Fair Credit Reporting Act that requires a credit bureau to reinvestigate any information in your file that is misleading, incorrect, or incomplete. Credit repair clinics want you to ask for reinvestigation again and again.

What would be the point of reinvestigating again and again?
The only point is to clog up the system so that, in the end, the credit bureaus will simply shrug their shoulders and give in. Is

that a loophole? I don't think so. Not to mention that this approach seldom meets with success. Plus, credit bureaus are very suspicious of reinvestigation requests that look as if they are sent from a credit repair clinic.

What else do credit repair clinics do?

They advise you to dispute practically everything in your credit file. That includes your Social Security number, your address, and even your name! Some clinics will go so far as to suggest that their customers take on a new identity and become entirely new people. This is certainly one way to get a clean slate, but one I hardly recommend. (In case you were wondering, under the new credit repair statutes, changing your identity to avoid debt is strictly against the law.)

PAYDAY LOAN COMPANIES

What are payday loans?

Payday loans (also called cash-advance loans, check-advance loans, postdated check loans, or deferred-deposit check loans) are cash-advance loans secured by a personal check minus a fee charged by the payday loan company. Fees charged for payday loans are usually a percentage of the face value of the check, or a fee charged per amount borrowed. The average fee for a payday loan is $20 to $25 per $100 borrowed, and is due in full on your next payday. Most lenders allow for the original loan to be rolled over to the next payday for an additional fee of $20 to $25 per $100 borrowed. Under the Truth in Lending Act, the cost of payday loans—like other types of credit—must be disclosed. Among other information, you must receive, in writing, the finance charge (a dollar amount) and the annual percentage rate, or APR (the cost of credit on a yearly basis).

How do payday loans work?

Let's say you write a postdated personal check for $120 (which includes a $20 finance fee) to borrow $100 for up to 14 days. The check-casher or payday lender agrees to hold the check until your next payday. At that time, depending on the particular plan, the lender deposits the check, or you redeem the check by paying the $120 in cash, or you roll over the check by paying a fee to extend the loan for another two weeks. In this example, the cost of the initial loan is a $20 finance charge. If you roll over the loan three times, the finance charge would climb to $80 to borrow $100. A payday loan can start a vicious cycle of borrowing from future earnings to pay today's bills.

REESTABLISHING CREDIT

I got into trouble with debt and am trying to fix my bad credit rating. How do I start over again?

It's human nature to want to wipe the slate clean. Unfortunately, this is not always possible. The most important thing is that you are facing your credit history—and that you clearly want to take steps to improve the situation.

If you haven't done so already, start at the very beginning. Get a copy of your credit report and study it carefully. Make sure that all the information contained in it is accurate and up to date.

The second step is to do whatever you can to try to pay some portion, if not all, of your delinquent accounts. This sends your creditors a clear message: You are not dodging your debts. You have a sincere desire to pay what you owe.

How about trying to establish credit again? Is this impossible?

No, it's not impossible, but it may take some time. Some good sources of information and advice are two excellent books about credit rebuilding published by Nolo Press, *Money Troubles* and *Credit Repair*.

What do creditors like to see as evidence that I'm able to handle money responsibly?

You need a record of stable employment and should have lived in your current house or apartment for at least six months. And though there are disadvantages, I would apply for a gas card, a department store card, or both. Because of their high interest rates, you won't want to make any major charges on these, but gas and department store cards are often considered good stepping-stones to establishing credit. And make sure you make timely payments every month! Remember, you are being given a second chance, and you don't want to slip up.

Do references from a bank help?

Yes. If I were starting to rebuild my credit after a period of not paying my bills on time, one of the first things I would do is open a checking or a savings account, or both. Creditors look at these accounts as solid evidence that you are able to handle money in a responsible way.

Can I try to take out a loan from a bank to reestablish my credit?

Sometimes this can be a very good idea, but make sure that the loan is a small one. Remember, you are trying to show your creditors that you are an honorable and consistent person who can pay your bills regularly over a long period of time. Credit is not a right. It is a privilege.

What about applying for a new credit card?

Ironically, you may find it's easier to get a credit card following a bankruptcy than with a simple history of late payments or arrears. Start with a gas, store, or secured credit card. If you have declared bankruptcy, be careful: You may be playing with fire if you apply for a credit card. You could find yourself in trouble once again.

My credit is bad, and as a result all the credit companies have turned me down. In the mail recently I got a solicitation from a company that offered me a "check guarantee" card for a small fee. Should I get it?

Probably not. A check guarantee card is issued by a bank or lending company and guarantees to a merchant checks that you write, up to a specific amount. I would advise you to stay away from these cards, since you will likely only be covered for the amount of money you have in your account anyway, and you could simply pay with cash and avoid the fee charged for use of the card. Better to look into a secured credit card.

What is a secured credit card, and where can I find one?

A secured credit card is just what it sounds like: a credit card secured by a cash deposit, usually of $300 or more. The bank issuing the card will generally extend a credit limit of up to 120 percent of your initial deposit. If for some reason you fail to pay your credit card bill, the savings institution will simply take the money you owe from your deposit. In the meantime, your security deposit earns interest, and, because the account will be reported to all the major credit bureaus, if you pay your bills in a timely fashion you will begin to build a good credit history. No one will know the account is secured—not even the credit bureaus.

Do you recommend secured credit cards?

Yes, I do. In fact, I recommend them even for people who are not in credit card trouble, since they are so safe. Of course, they are especially useful if you are trying to reestablish good credit after a period of delinquency.

Are the fees and interest rates for secured credit cards the same as for credit cards that are not secured?

Consumers who have had trouble with their credit in the past may find that the price of obtaining a secured credit card is somewhat higher than it would be for other people. Generally, there is a onetime processing fee of $19 for a secured Visa or MasterCard. The annual percentage rate for balances on purchases and for cash advances is usually quite high, about 19.9 percent (fixed). You may also find annual fees for secured cards in the neighborhood of $39. Additional deposits will increase your credit limit with a good payment record, but your credit line may increase after 12 months even if you don't make additional deposits.

All in all, a secured credit card may be less convenient and a little more costly than other cards, because the amount of your credit line will be limited by how much you have deposited, but these two factors may help to keep your spending—and debt—under control. If you've had trouble with credit card debt in the past, a secured credit card may be just what you need.

Following a period of bad credit, I have recently repaired my problems with credit card companies. Am I now going to run into trouble if I apply for a mortgage?

The answer is probably not. However, with mortgage lenders, as with credit card companies, your case will be helped considerably if you can prove that your past troubled credit history was directly caused by circumstances that are either beyond your control or unlikely to happen again—illness, a messy divorce, a lost job. If you have declared bankruptcy, your chances to get approved for a mortgage increase significantly if the bankruptcy was resolved at least two years earlier and you've established good credit since then.

BORROWING TO REPAY DEBT

Many of us are tempted to borrow from our future to get what we want today. This can be dangerous, especially if you do not understand the financial ramifications of your actions. The following questions and answers will help you to make informed decisions about the potentially risky practice of borrowing to pay off credit card debt.

401(k) OR RETIREMENT PLAN

Can I borrow from my 401(k) to pay off back taxes, a student loan, or my credit card debts?
Probably. Many employers will allow you to borrow up to 50 percent of the money in your 401(k) or retirement plan, up to $50,000, to pay for things that qualify, including a house, a college education, and sometimes debt repayment. This loan, you should know, does not come interest-free; interest rates are set by your company. They are generally reasonable. Typically, they are about 2 percent above the prime rate, the basic interest rate set by the government.

What are the advantages of borrowing from my 401(k)?

One of the biggest supposed advantages of borrowing money from your 401(k) is that since you are effectively borrowing your *own* money, from yourself, the interest you pay, as well as the principal, goes right back into your account. You have five years to pay back the money you borrow. Please read on to see why I don't want you to do this.

If I borrow money from my 401(k), won't this prevent my 401(k) from increasing in value?

Possibly. Depending on what the markets are doing you could be losing out on some of the growth potential of your money. But if you are paying 18.5 or 21 percent interest on your credit cards, for example, and can't transfer your balance to a lower-rate card, you might actually save money by borrowing from yourself at 8 or 9 percent.

Are there other disadvantages to borrowing money from my 401(k)?

Yes, there are several. One major disadvantage: If you happen to leave your job or get fired, the money you borrowed will be due in one lump sum within days or weeks of your departure. If you do not have the money to repay the loan at that time, your remaining loan amount will be taxable to you as ordinary income. If you are younger than $59\frac{1}{2}$ at that time, you will also pay a 10 percent federal penalty.

A more universal and less-well-known disadvantage is this: If you borrow money from your 401(k) to pay off your credit card debt, you will be taxed twice on the loan amount. Here's how this works. The money you borrow is money you contributed to your retirement plan before taxes; the money you use to pay off the loan is after-tax money. Later, when you withdraw your 401(k) money for retirement, it will be taxed again. If at all possible, if you borrow from your 401(k), please try your best to make your normal contributions as well as your loan payments, or your long-term loss may be too great.

But let's look at what a 401(k) loan can do to your retirement savings. Say you are 35 years old, make $40,000 a year, and have a 401(k) balance of $20,000. You contribute $2,400, or 6 percent of your salary, per year, and your employer match is $1,200. Assume that you get an annual return of 8 percent on your account. If you continue saving at this rate until age 65, your retirement nest egg will be about $624,000.

You decide to take a loan from your 401(k) to pay off your credit card debt. You take out a $10,000 loan on your 401(k), with five years to repay it. But you can't afford to continue making contributions while you repay it. What happens? When you reach age 65, your account will be worth $458,673. That difference of roughly $127,000 in savings translates into a loss of $7,620 a year in retirement income, assuming returns of 6 percent. That's about $635 a month, which is quite a chunk of cash. Are you convinced?

Are there preliminary charges for a 401(k) loan?
Sometimes. With a 401(k) loan, fees are variable. Some employers will charge you for taking out the loan, and some won't. Some make you pay a fee of up to $100 just to fill out the paperwork, and some charge a yearly fee while the loan is outstanding.

Is taking out a 401(k) loan easy?
Yes, fairly easy. You may have to fill out a form with your human resources department, or you may be able to apply over the phone with the financial company that manages your 401(k). Loans from either source take time to process, however, so if you're desperate, comparison shop. Ask your employer and a lender how long a 401(k) loan and a home

equity loan will take to process, respectively, and when you will have the money in hand.

If I take out a 401(k) loan, who decides which of my investments within the 401(k) are sold off?

Who decides which of your investments are cashed in depends on your company's internal policies. Some companies will let you decide; others will make a decision for you. If you have any doubts about how this works in your company, ask the benefits adviser in your human resources department. If you do have a choice of which investments to liquidate, I would start liquidating money that is parked in either money-market funds or bond funds and then move on to your worst-performing equity funds. If you're unsure of how your equity funds have been performing, request a summary of the latest returns of your investments in the 401(k) plan from your human resources department. Check your funds' overall returns for one year, three years, five years, and, if available, ten years. See which funds have had the highest and most consistent returns overall, and which have had the lowest returns. Start liquidating the ones with the lowest returns, and move up the list from there.

What happens if I cannot pay back the loan to my 401(k)?

If you can't pay back the amount that you borrowed in five years' time, your loan will be considered to be in default. At that point, your employer and the IRS consider the outstanding balance as a taxable withdrawal, and you will pay taxes on the money as if it were ordinary income. If you're under age 59½, you may also have to pay a 10 percent early-withdrawal penalty. This is a potentially vicious circle, since it often obliges individual consumers to cash in even more of their 401(k) plan assets—which are also taxable and subject to the same possible early-withdrawal penalty—to pay the loan.

HOME EQUITY LOAN

What about taking out a home equity loan to pay off my credit card debt?

A home equity loan is another option, with its own advantages and disadvantages, but I believe that the disadvantages are far fewer than with borrowing from a 401(k). Like a loan from a 401(k), a home equity loan may well carry a lower interest rate than your credit card does; unlike a 401(k) loan, often that interest is tax-deductible, so you can convert a high-interest, non-tax-deductible debt to a lower-interest, tax-deductible debt. The problem is this: If you do not have your credit card spending under control, before you know it you can easily find that you have charged your cards to the max again *and* have a home equity loan to repay. If you do this, you will effectively have doubled your debt load and put your home at risk of foreclosure.

If I have $80,000 equity in my home, can I take out an $80,000 home equity loan?

No. You can't automatically get a home equity loan equal to the amount of equity you have in your home. Most banks will allow you to borrow only up to 80 percent of the value of your house, less all current mortgage balances. If your house is worth $200,000, for example, 80 percent of its value is $160,000. Subtract the balance you owe on your mortgage— let's say that's $120,000—and this gives you the amount you can get as a home equity loan (if you qualify): in this case, $40,000. You qualify for a home equity loan depending on the amount of equity you have in your home *and* on your ability to meet your other debts and financial obligations.

I have a friend whose bank let him borrow more than 80 percent of the value of his home.

Some banks want you to borrow 80 percent or more of the value of your home, and it can turn out to be quite costly for you. Most mortgage companies that lend more than 80 percent will make you pay what is called private mortgage insurance, or PMI, which will add quite a bit to the loan. (Please see *Ask Suze...About Real Estate* for more on PMI.) So it's best if you can stick to the straight 80 percent loans, which are based on what lenders think you can comfortably afford.

Are there fees to take out a home equity loan?

Again, sometimes. Some can carry no fees except for an appraisal on your home (at a cost of $200 to $300), and some lenders will charge fees up front to take out the loan or for the paperwork, which can add another $100 or $200 to the bill. But if you look carefully, you should be able to find a home equity loan with no fees, no points, and a very small appraisal fee, if any.

What happens if I cannot pay back my home equity loan?

It is quite possible that the bank will foreclose on your home, which means that it can be sold to repay the loan.

What is an equity line of credit?

An equity line of credit will not give you a lump sum but will enable you to borrow money as you need it against the value of your house.

How is an equity line of credit different from a home equity loan?

A home equity line of credit usually has a rate that varies according to what market interest rates are doing, while a home equity loan has a fixed interest rate. Also, with an equity line of credit, you do not have to pay back principal each month if you don't want to; you can pay just the interest. So the payback period for an equity line of credit is not set. A home equity loan, on the other hand, works pretty much like a regular mortgage. You get a fixed interest rate and pay back the loan over a set period of time, usually five to fifteen years. So make sure you're extremely disciplined if you consider an equity line of credit.

BORROWING FROM YOUR 401(K) VS. A HOME EQUITY LOAN: WHICH IS BETTER?

	401(K) LOAN	HOME EQUITY LOAN
Tax-deductible	No	Probably
Payback period	5 years	5 to 15 years
Subject to income tax if not paid back	Yes	Possibly
Due/Payable if you leave current employer	Yes	No
Giving up potential growth	Yes	No
Double taxation	Yes	No

LOAN AMOUNT: $10,000

	401(K) LOAN	HOME EQUITY LOAN
Monthly payment	$208	$208
Number of payments	60	60
Total paid	$12,455	$12,455
Total interest paid	$2,455	$2,455
Tax savings (at 28%)	0	$687

ASK SUZE

Borrowing from a 401(k) vs. Taking a Home Equity Loan: A Comparison

Which makes more financial sense: taking out a home equity loan or borrowing from my 401(k)?

In my opinion, taking out a home equity loan is, hands down, the better choice. Take a look at the chart on page 95, and see how the two choices measure up.

Now consider the actual numbers. Let's examine what it means to borrow $10,000 at 9 percent interest (assuming a 28 percent tax bracket). In both scenarios, the payback period is five years.

Please note: This does not take into consideration the double taxation of a 401(k) loan when repaid. If you can avoid a loan from your 401(k) plan, please do.

Collection Agencies

I am in deep trouble with debt. I can't pay my credit card bills or my car loan. Is somebody going to put me in jail?

No. A creditor can't put you in jail because of debt. But it can turn your account over to a collection agency, take you to court to sue for the amount that is due, garnish your wages, or foreclose on your house. Credit card companies can be really tough when it comes to collecting money.

Aren't credit card companies regulated as to how they collect a debt?

No. It's only when a credit card company, or primary creditor, turns a debt over to an outside collection agency that debt collection is regulated.

Collection agencies *are* federally regulated, but there are few laws that govern how a primary creditor, such as a bank or a credit card company, gets its money back.

How long do I have before a credit card company turns my account over to a collection agency?

Typically, three to six months. Here's how it works. When your credit card account is two weeks late, you will usually receive a friendly reminder in the mail or sometimes even a phone call from the credit card company. If you haven't paid the minimum due on your account after two months, it's very likely you'll get another letter, this time less friendly, and perhaps several more phone calls. At this point, your card might be frozen—which means you can't make any more purchases until the matter has been resolved to the credit card company's satisfaction. After three or four months of delinquency—meaning that you haven't responded satisfactorily to letters and phone calls, or that you promised to pay and you didn't—a lot of creditors will consider your account a "bad debt." This is when the collection agencies come in.

What do the collection agencies want from me?

Collection agencies have one purpose: Getting you to pay back the money you owe. Usually they work on commission, receiving between 10 percent and 60 percent of what they manage to collect. Sometimes they will turn their cases over to a lawyer, who will draft a letter warning you that if you do not pay off your delinquent balance at once, you will be sued and taken to court. Once your account has gone to a collection agency, you have lost the opportunity to negotiate with the credit card company. If you call the card company, they will simply refer you to the collection agency.

What if I don't hear from the collection agency for a while? Does this mean I'm off the hook?
Probably not. Some collections begin years after the inception of a debt.

A collection agency contacted me, demanding immediate payment of a debt I know I do not owe. What should I do?
Be on the lookout for dishonest bill collectors, and never make a payment on a debt that you feel is not valid. Instead, within 30 days of receiving such a call or letter, make a request in writing that the collection agency verify the validity of the debt. Further, ask that the collection agency send written verification that this debt was incurred by you. Recently, the courts have upheld rulings that demands for immediate payment in an initial contact by a collection agency are in violation of the Fair Debt Collection Practices Act (see the following question).

I am being pursued by a collection agency. Are there any laws governing how a collection agency can behave?
Yes. The Fair Debt Collection Practices Act (FDCPA) was passed to protect customers from being shaken down by collection companies. This act restricts the tactics they may use. Please note: The FDCPA applies to outside collection agencies, the ones that most credit card companies hire after their own attempts have failed, and not to the collection department within the card company or other lender.

What are collection agencies not allowed to do?

As a result of the FDCPA, collectors cannot phone your home so often as to harass you. They cannot call before 8 A.M. or after 9 P.M. They cannot threaten you or use obscene language. They cannot call you directly if they know you are being represented by an attorney, and they cannot call you at work if they know your employer prohibits such calls. They cannot call your friends, your neighbors, or the people you work with and reveal your financial situation.

Can a collection agency obtain information on my whereabouts from government records, such as Social Security records or my tax returns?

No, a collection agency cannot make use of government records. But an original creditor can gather information from a state motor vehicle department about registration of a car, from your voter registration records, from the post office, or from a utility company or a bank, in order to locate you.

My collection agency does everything it is not supposed to do. Can I sue?

Yes, you can sue a collection agency, but a better first step might be to use the provisions of the FDCPA to warn your collection agency that it is acting in defiance of the law. What you should do is to write a letter telling the collection agency to stay away from you, to leave you alone, and to cease all communications with you. In this letter, inform the collection agency that under provision 15 of the U.S. Code, section 1692c, this letter constitutes your formal notice to stop all future communications with you except for the reasons specifically set forth in the federal law.

I have written a letter like the one above, but I'm still being harassed. What can I do?

Contact the Federal Trade Commission and register a formal complaint.

If you can prove continued harassment, the collection agency is open to a lawsuit—one you could win if you have the proper documentation or proof. There have been several successful suits against collectors where the consumer won in court.

Do I have any other legal recourse against a collection agency?

If you think that the collection agency may be behaving in a way that you suspect is illegal, write a letter to the Federal Trade Commission (for the address, see page 63), including as many details as possible. Send a copy to your state attorney general's office, your local consumer-protection office, or both. You might also consider sending a copy to the legal department of the credit card company that started the ball rolling in the first place. If this fails, contact the Association of Credit and Collection Professionals at P.O. Box 39106, Minneapolis, MN 55439, (952) 926-6547. Its members agree to conduct their business in a professional manner.

STATUTES OF LIMITATIONS

If I choose not to pay my debt for whatever reason, how long do I have to run and hide from the credit card companies in case they sue me?

The answer depends on the state in which you live and what kind of debt you have. In every state, the statute of limitations for credit card debt begins to tick from the date you failed to make a payment that was due, as long as you never make another payment on that credit card account. If your state's statute of limitations on credit card debt is seven years and your last payment was due on January 10, then the statute of limitations on your debt will run out seven years from that January 10, assuming you haven't made another payment.

Say I charge $5,000 on my credit card, and the due date is January 10. I don't pay in January but I pay the minimum amount in February. Then, in March, I get a statement saying the next payment is due March 10, but I don't make that payment. I never make a payment again. Does the statute run from January 10 or from March 10?

The statute will start to run as of March 10. Be careful in making additional payments, because they start the legal clock ticking all over again. In some states, simply making an oral promise to pay resets the clock. In other states, the promise to repay must be in writing and signed by you.

How long does the statute of limitations for credit card debt last in the various states?

Here's the list, as of the year 2003:

Alabama	3 years
Alaska	6 years
Arizona	6 years
Arkansas	3 years
California	4 years
Colorado	4 years
Connecticut	6 years
Delaware	3 years
District of Columbia	3 years
Florida	4 years

Georgia	4 years
Hawaii	6 years
Idaho	4 years
Illinois	5 years
Indiana	6 years
Iowa	5 years
Kansas	3 years
Kentucky	5 years
Louisiana	3 years
Maine	6 years
Maryland	3 years
Massachusetts	6 years
Michigan	6 years
Minnesota	6 years
Mississippi	3 years
Missouri	5 years
Montana	5 years
Nebraska	4 years
Nevada	4 years
New Hampshire	3 years
New Jersey	6 years
New Mexico	4 years
New York	6 years
North Carolina	3 years
North Dakota	6 years
Ohio	15 years
Oklahoma	3 years
Oregon	6 years
Pennsylvania	6 years
Rhode Island	10 years
South Carolina	3 years
South Dakota	6 years
Tennessee	6 years

Texas	4 years
Utah	4 years
Vermont	6 years
Virginia	3 years
Washington	3 years
West Virginia	5 years
Wisconsin	6 years
Wyoming	8 years

I am pretty sure the statute of limitations on my debt has run out. Why do I keep getting calls from a collection agency?

If an original creditor or bank becomes aware that the statute of limitations on a debt is about to run out, it will sometimes sell the debt to a collection agency. The collection agency will take a chance that you do not know that the statute of limitations is running—or has run—out, and will try to collect anyway. It's a good idea always to be aware of statutes of limitations on your debt.

Under what circumstances can a state's statute of limitations be extended?

A statute of limitations will be extended for the length of time you are out of state; in prison; or, if you are a minor and somehow get yourself into debt, by the length of time it will take you to reach age 18.

STUDENT LOANS

What do you think about student loans?

If you have no other way of paying for college or graduate

school, I think taking out a student loan is one of the best and most honorable investments you can make for your future. In my opinion, student loans fall in the category of "good debt." Why? Because you are borrowing money to invest in yourself and your future.

If I take out a student loan, will I get a tax deduction?

Yes. You can now deduct interest payments on your student loans without regard to how long you have been making interest payments, subject to certain income qualifications. (Before the Tax Relief and Reconciliation Act of 2001 went into effect, you could only deduct the first 60 months of interest payments.) In 2006, you can deduct up to $2,500 of student loan interest.

Is there just one kind of student loan, or are there many different kinds?

There are several kinds of student loans, which are described at *http://studentaid.ed.gov/*. Probably the oldest and best known is a Perkins loan. With Perkins loans, the U.S. government lends a certain amount of money to a college, which in turn lends it to students who need it. (For more on borrowing to pay for college, please see *Ask Suze...About Planning for Your Future.*) The Perkins loan carries a very low interest rate—5 percent. Then again, it is one of the smallest loans out there: It has a ceiling of $4,000 per year, and no more than $20,000 over the course of your undergraduate studies. If you are a graduate or a postgraduate student, you can borrow up to $6,000 per year, with a cap of $40,000.

How long do I have to pay off my Perkins loan?

You may have to begin repaying your Perkins loan nine months after you leave college, and you may have up to ten years after that to pay off the full amount. Colleges often sell these loans, with their outstanding balances, to banks. This doesn't mean much to you, except that you will now be making payments to the bank rather than the college.

I need a little more money than a Perkins loan can give me. What are my options?

You might consider a Stafford loan. A Stafford—sometimes known as a Federal Family Education Loan (FFEL), a Ford loan, or a direct loan, depending on whether the lender is the college, a bank, or the federal government—exists to make up the difference between the cost of college tuition and the expected family contribution, or EFC. The EFC is the amount the college believes a family should be able to pay after it has crunched the family's financials. Each dependent student— either at a two-year or a four-year institution—can borrow between $3,500 and $5,500, depending on their year of study, at an interest rate that became fixed in 2006 at 6.8 percent. The maximum total a dependent student (one who has access to parental support) can borrow is $23,000. You begin repaying the loan six months after you leave college, and you have ten years to pay back the entire amount, though often there is room for negotiation.

To apply for a Stafford loan, you must fill out a form. If the lender is a bank rather than a college, you are required to submit a letter from your college stating your eligibility.

Finally, you should be aware that there are two forms of Stafford loans: subsidized and unsubsidized.

What is the difference between a subsidized and an unsubsidized Stafford loan?

If you receive a subsidized Stafford loan, you will not be charged any interest until you begin to repay the loan (six months after you leave college). Until then, the government assumes responsibility for your interest payments. With an unsubsidized Stafford, you (not the government) are responsible for the interest payments while you are at college and for the first six months after you leave. This doesn't mean that you have to pay interest every month; you can defer the interest payments and add them to the principal to be repaid after you have graduated.

My folks have talked to me about taking out a PLUS loan. What is this?

PLUS stands for Parents' Loans for Undergraduate Students. It is a loan with a fairly low interest rate (it became a fixed rate of 8.5 percent in 2006) that will cover the difference between the cost of attendance (COA), and the amount of financial aid that you will be receiving. The cost of attendance is the total amount it costs a student to go to school. For full-time students this includes tuition, fees, room and board, allowances for books, supplies, transportation, costs related to dependent care of disability, and miscellaneous expenses. The yearly limit on a PLUS loan is equal to the cost of attendance minus any other financial aid you receive. For example, if your COA is $6,000 and you receive $4,000 in financial aid, your parents could borrow up to but no more than $2,000.

I want to apply for a student loan, but my credit rating isn't great. Will I have problems?

Oddly enough, you probably won't. If you—or your family—have had a checkered history of bill paying or even a bankruptcy, it will not work against you. The only thing that could count against you is if you have ever defaulted on a previous student loan. The only qualifications for a Stafford or a Perkins loan are:

- need
- a high school diploma or GED
- enrollment or acceptance for enrollment as a regular student working toward a degree or certificate in an eligible program
- U.S. citizenship or eligible noncitizen status
- a valid Social Security number

Please note: If you are a veteran, the child of a veteran who died or was permanently disabled in battle, a nursing student, a pharmacy student, or a Native American, special grants and dispensations are available to you. Check with your college or university.

Who exactly grants and manages my loan—the Department of Education or a bank?

Who your loan holder will be depends on the type of loan you take out. If you take out a Perkins loan, your loan will be managed by the school that lends you the money or by an institution that the school assigns to service the loan. If you take out a direct loan, the funds for your loan are lent to you directly by the U.S. government and it will be managed by the Direct Loan Servicing Center at the U.S. Department of Education. If you borrow a FFEL, the funds for your loan are lent to you from a bank, credit union, or other lender that participates in the FFEL program and will be managed by your lender or its servicing agent. Your lender or the Direct Loan Servicing Center *(www.dlservicer.ed.gov)* will provide you with additional information about your loan.

STUDENT LOAN CONSOLIDATION

What does it mean to consolidate my student loans?

In effect, consolidating means taking all your loans, bundling them into one loan, and getting a new fixed rate. You can also get a longer repayment schedule—although, of course, I would advise you against doing this; in fact, I would recommend that you take any monthly savings you reap from the lower interest rate and pay off your student loans or (even better) your credit card debt more quickly. To consolidate your student loans, apply online at *www.loanconsolidation.ed.gov* or call (800) 557-7392.

Should I consolidate my student loans?

Though the interest rates on Stafford and PLUS loans became fixed in 2006, interest rates on those loans taken out before 2006 remain variable, and will continue to change annually. Depending on the curent interest rate environment, you may want to consider consolidating your student loans, if you have never consolidated them before. New annual interest rates on variable rate student loans are set once a year, on July 1. If you are thinking about consolidating at a time when interest rates in general have been falling, depending on your situation and where you are in the calendar year, you might want to wait to see whether the new rates on July 1 will be lower than the current ones. Here's what to do. If you are just a short period of time away—let's say it is February or March—instead of consolidating now, hold off until May 1 and check out the interest rate the government is paying on the 91-day Treasury bill. That's right—the rate on the 91-day Treasury bill is the rate to which student loan rates are tied. (You can check T-bill rates by logging on to *www.publicdebt.treas.gov/servlet/OFBills*.) There are formulas that govern how loan rates work. In the case of Stafford loans, for example, the new loan rate, announced on July 1, will be equal to the May T-bill rate plus 2.3 percent. The new PLUS loan rate will be equal to the May T-bill rate plus 3.1 percent. If doing the math leads you to conclude that the

July rates will be lower than the current rates, wait until the new rates are announced, then consolidate. If you think they will stay the same or go higher, don't wait; check the current rate and consider consolidating now.

What should I do if I am still within the grace period?

If you have just graduated and you are still within the grace period—the period during which you do not yet have to pay back the loan—wait until about five weeks *before* your grace period is up to apply for a loan consolidation. That way, you take full advantage of your grace period but still consolidate your payments as soon as possible once it has ended.

POSTPONING OR CANCELING STUDENT LOAN PAYMENTS

If I really cannot make my payments, is there anything I can do?

Yes. Options range from having your loan canceled, which means you will not ever have to pay it back (this is almost impossible), to getting either a deferment or a forbearance. What you can or cannot do depends on what kind of loan you have and the reason you cannot pay.

Under what circumstance can a student loan be canceled?

A student loan can be canceled if you are permanently disabled or die, or under certain other circumstances that also apply to deferment. Please read on.

How do I cancel my loan?

If you have called the loan holder and you feel you qualify for a cancellation, you must apply for it. Call the Department of Education's Debt Collection Service Information Center at

(800) 621-3115 and request an application. Fill it out and return it with all the paperwork the department will request.

What is a deferment?

A deferment simply means that you defer the loan repayment—wait until a later date to make it. During that time, in most cases, no interest accrues.

Under what conditions can a loan be deferred?

Conditions will vary with the kind of loan you have and when you obtained it, but in general your loan can be deferred if you, your spouse, or one of your dependants becomes disabled; if you go back to school part-time; if, for whatever reason, you are currently unemployed; or if you have young children. If you have a federal loan and are suffering an economic hardship, you can probably get a deferment of up to three years. You are automatically eligible if you are on Supplemental Security Income or are getting any kind of public assistance. If you join the U.S. military you may qualify for a deferment or even, under certain circumstances, a cancellation. You may also qualify to have your loan deferred or canceled if you get a job in law enforcement, become a teacher working with the underprivileged or needy, or get a job in a health-care profession in a part of the country where there is a shortage of health-care workers. You can also get a deferment or a cancellation if you decide to perform community service, such as serving in the Peace Corps. Finally, you can get a deferment if you enroll in a rehabilitation program for the disabled. Again, please note that each situation is different. Call the holder of your loan and ask under what circumstances you would qualify for a deferment of your loan.

If I have been in default on my loan, can I still apply for a deferment?

No. If you are in default, you will not be able to get a deferment. If you have merely been late in making payments a few times and are not in default, you may be eligible for what is called a retroactive deferment.

How do I defer my loan?

You have to apply for a deferment. Call the holder of your loan and explain why you think you qualify for a deferment. The loan holder will send you the appropriate paperwork.

If I get a deferment, how long will I be allowed to defer my payments?

Usually for about six months to one year. The economic-hardship deferment is for three years, but, as always, each case will be different depending on the kind of deferment, what kind of loan you have, and when you got it.

If I get a deferment and I need to apply for another one, can I?

Yes. Each time you are granted a deferment, the holder of the loan will let you know how long that deferment will last and when you should reapply, if necessary.

In a deferment, does the interest on my loan keep accumulating?

In most cases, no.

If I do not qualify for a deferment or a cancellation, is there anything else I can do?

Yes. You can apply for a forbearance. A forbearance is very much like a deferment in that you are allowed to put off making payments for a certain length of time. But with a forbearance, interest *always* continues to accrue during the time you are not making payments. Also, with a forbearance, it does not matter when you obtained the loan or what kind of loan it is, which makes a forbearance far easier to get than a deferment.

I have been in default and I know I cannot get a deferment. Can I get a forbearance?

Yes. You can get a forbearance even if you have been in default.

If I have a number of loans, do I have to get a forbearance on each of them?

No. The number of loans on which you apply for a forbearance will depend on how much money you are short. Since the interest continues to accumulate while you are not making payments on these loans, you have to be very careful. If you have many loans, apply for a forbearance on the lowest-interest-rate loans first. It may seem better to postpone the higher-interest-rate loans, but in the long run it is not. Remember that the interest is still adding up.

My loan payments are currently more than 20 percent of my gross income. Can I get a forbearance?

Yes. When your loan payments total 20 percent or more of your gross income, your loan holder is actually required to give you a forbearance if you want one.

How long will a forbearance last?

The length of time varies according to the loan holder, but it is usually up to three years.

If I apply for a deferment, forbearance, or a cancellation of my loan, can I stop making payments at that time?

No. When you are applying for a deferment, cancellation, or forbearance, you must continue to make payments until you are notified that the request has been granted. If you don't, you may end up in default. Keep a copy of any request form you submit, and document all contacts with the organization that holds or manages your loan.

DEFAULTING ON A STUDENT LOAN

More than 20 years ago, I took out a student loan. I've never repaid it and I've never heard from anyone. Will the same be true for my children if they do not pay back their student loans?

I'm afraid not. It used to be the case that if you took out a student loan and did not pay it back, you might not ever hear from anyone. But that is no longer true. If your children do not pay back the money they borrow, they will hear about it immediately and will suffer financial consequences in a big way.

When exactly am I considered to be in default?

You are not usually considered to be in default until you have not made student loan payments or had any contact with the loan holder to apply for a deferment, forbearance, or cancellation for at least six months.

If I have not repaid my student loans for years and the interest and penalties have mounted up, can I negotiate to get those penalties dropped or reduced?

You can try, but your chances are not good. To my knowledge, student loan holders seldom successfully negotiate or make a deal.

I am about to default on my student loans. What will happen to me if I do?

If you do default on your student loans, your lender or the agency that holds your loan, by the authority of the state and of the federal government, may take action to recover the money, including suing you and/or notifying national credit bureaus of your default. This may affect your credit rating for up to seven years, making it very difficult to borrow from a bank to buy a car or a house, or rent an apartment, among other things. If you are working or ever do work, up to 10 to 15 percent of your wages may be garnished, and if you are due to receive a tax refund, it can be taken to pay off your student loans. If you decide to return to school, you will not be entitled to receive any more federal student aid.

Is there a way for me to get out of default?

Yes—by making 9 out of 10 consecutive monthly payments on your loan. Not only will you then be able to apply for a deferment, you can also request that your default be cleared from your credit report.

I am in default. I want to pay off my student loan, but I cannot afford the current monthly amount that is due. Will my lender adjust the amount for me?

By law, you are not required to pay more on your student loans than you can reasonably afford. Gather all your financial paperwork, call your lender, and ask about what is called a reasonable and affordable repayment plan. Depending on your financial situation, your lender could allow you to pay as little as $5 a month.

What happens if I am granted this reasonable and affordable plan?

If you stay on schedule and make at least six monthly payments in a row, you will be eligible for new federal student loans. After 9 out of 10 monthly payments, you will no longer be in default. Then you will be eligible to apply for a deferral.

I am currently in default on two student loans but not on a third. Can I consolidate my loans?
Yes, you can. In fact, if you were to refinance or consolidate your loans, you would no longer be in default on those two loans.

WAGE GARNISHMENT

If I default on a student loan and I am working, does the Department of Education have legal authority to garnish my wages?
Yes. And not only the Department of Education but also the agencies that guarantee your loans. They have the right to take up to 15 percent of your wages.

I thought I had to be sued and get a court judgment in order for my wages to be garnished.
That is true of all loans except student loans. If you default on any other kind of loan, your creditors must get a court judgment against you, after which they can garnish up to 25 percent of your wages.

Will I know in advance if my wages are going to be garnished?
You will be notified beforehand. The Department of Education is obliged to let you know in writing 30 days before the garnishment date. It must tell you how much you owe, how you may enter into a repayment schedule so your wages are not garnished, and how you can obtain a hearing on this garnishment process to try to stop it.

How long do I have to respond to this letter?
You have approximately 15 days to respond, and your response must be in writing.

If the Department of Education is going to garnish my wages, at what point will it let my employer know?
The Department of Education will let your employer know it is going to garnish your wages about 20 business days after you receive its notice. It assumes you will receive the notice by five business days after the date they mailed it.

If I have just started a new job after not working for the past year, can my wages be garnished?
Yes. However, if you were fired or laid off and did not return to work for a full year, you can object to this garnishment and you may win.

I barely make enough to live on now. How can my wages be garnished?
If you do not earn at least 30 times the federal minimum wage per week, your wages cannot be garnished.

How many days can I be in default before my wages can be garnished?
You can be in default about 225 days before your wages can be garnished.

I have been in default for some time, and I seem to have slipped through the cracks. When is the statute of limitations up?
Never. If you haven't paid your student loan, you remain responsible for it and for any interest on it, too.

If I default and the Department of Education comes after me, what can they get?

Almost everything: your bank account, your car, and any other property and/or assets you own—as well as garnishing your wages.

If I am being harassed by a collection agency because I'm in default on a student loan, what should I do?

Call the Deputy Director of Debt Collections at (202) 377-3258.

STUDENT LOANS AND BANKRUPTCY

I have been told that if I claim bankruptcy I will not be able to get rid of my student loan. Is that true?

That is true. No student loan can be dismissed because of bankruptcy, no matter when it was taken out or when it comes due. The *only* exception to this rule is if paying back a student loan will cause you what is considered undue hardship. But bankruptcy courts have very strict definitions of undue hardship. In many cases, if you meet those definitions, you would also qualify to have your loan canceled—a far better choice.

If I file for Chapter 13 bankruptcy, can I include my student loan payments in my repayment plan?

Yes, but be careful. Chapter 13 bankruptcy allows an individual who has consumer (household) debts to make a plan to pay creditors, but there are limits to the amount of debt you can include, and other restrictions. Also, under Chapter 13 some of your creditors will get back only part of the amount you owe them and, essentially, the debts will be discharged—but this is not true of student loans. If you file for Chapter 13 and choose to pay back only a small amount per month on your student loans, you will still owe the balance at the end of Chapter 13 bankruptcy.

AUTOMOBILE DEBT

Why are you not a fan of car leasing?
When you lease a car, you take on a monthly expense that, in most circumstances, you will continue to have to pay for the rest of your life. Here is why: With leasing, you do not own the car you are driving; you are paying a monthly fee merely to use that automobile for a few years. At the end of the leasing period, you either have to give back the car or purchase it for a predetermined price—a price that is usually set in such a way that it makes no sense for you to go ahead and purchase it. That's because these days, the leasing companies entice you with a lower monthly fee to draw you in and then they make up their profits with an inflated *residual price*—the price you would have to pay to buy the car outright—at the end of the lease. So what you normally do after the lease period is up is turn in your leased auto to the dealer and lease another. And then what do you do? You do it again and again—for the rest of your life.

If I have lost my job and cannot make my lease payments on my car, is there any way to get out of the lease?
To get out of your lease, here are your options. You can:

- Buy the car outright or finance it.
- Sell it for as much as possible and pay that amount plus any additional amount you may still owe to the lease company.
- Try to find someone to assume the lease obligations.

If you cannot sell your car outright, you may want to try to find someone who will assume your lease payments. However, keep in mind that when a person assumes a lease from you, it *still* does not mean that *you* are off the hook! If the new leaser does not make the payments, the lending company will come after *you*. So be careful with whom you make your agreement to assume the lease.

If you decide to sell the car on your own, you still have to come up with the difference between what you owe the lease company and what you sold the car for. And what happens if you do not have that money? You're in trouble again. Therefore, to make sure you don't find yourself short, you need to prepare for this unknown *when you first consider leasing* if money is tight for you at that time. When you have leased your car, see if you can also get approved for what's called a *signature loan,* for about $10,000. If you have been approved for a car lease, you can usually qualify for this other loan. This loan will give you the backup to help you get through an unforeseen crisis. Here's how.

Let's say, again, you have leased a car and an unforeseen problem happens and you can no longer make the car payments. Before you return the car to the dealer or lender, see if you can sell it on your own. The way you can do this is to run an ad to sell your car for the payoff *only*—do not try to escalate the price to make money, for it will not happen. (You want to attract buyers who can solve your problem, not scare them away.) When a potential buyer makes an offer on your car, negotiate the best price you can in a nice manner. Hopefully, you will arrive at a sum that will help you pay off the lender with what you've negotiated plus your signature loan. If you have any portion of the signature loan left over, pay it back to the bank immediately. You have now eliminated a large car payment for 48 to 60 months, and the lease is closed or, more important, paid as agreed upon according to the lease's terms.

If you decide just to return the leased car to the leasing company without trying to repay the balance on your lease, be aware that there is a big downside. After you return the car, the company may try to sell the car at an auction. Even if the car sells at auction, however, you will still owe the difference between the balance on your lease at that time and the auction proceeds for the car. Sometimes the company even charges you more for penalties and recapture of depreciation. It is probable that your lease company has a used-car lot. The person who runs that used-car lot can go to that auction and buy your car for, say, $4,000. The problem is that you owed $12,000 on the car at the time you had to give it back. So even with the $4,000 from the sale of the car at auction, you still owe $8,000 to the lease company, and now you have no wheels to get around.

In the meantime, the lease company has your car back on its used-car lot, and the car is up for sale. The company can probably sell it quickly for $10,000. Between the $8,000 you still owe and the profit the company is collecting on the sale of the car, someone is making out like a bandit, and it is not you. You are still paying for a car that *you* do not even have. This is what is known as a bummer.

I've heard that leasing is better than buying a car because of the tax write-offs.

I know that some financial experts want you to ignore all the dangers of leasing. They will show you the tax advantages of leasing over buying and why, in your case, you should lease rather than buy. I do not care about the tax advantages for most people. They are not significant compared to your overriding need to know how you are going to handle any unforeseen financial crisis in your life.

Say you are in a car accident or the car happens to get stolen. As we said earlier, the deal you made with your leasing company most likely means you will owe more than the car's current market value, which is all your insurance company may reimburse you for. You can buy extra insurance, called *gap insurance,* to protect you against this, and maybe your lease deal included it. But do you know for sure?

Many people who lease just love getting those great tax write-offs for the first year and also love how they look driving a fancy car. However, I have watched as some have become absolutely clinically depressed after they saw their car being carted away because they could no longer make their lease payments and yet were still responsible for those payments.

CHILD-SUPPORT DEBT

My ex-husband has not paid child support in three years, and I need the money. How do I find him and collect?

The federal government and each of the 50 states maintain what is known as a parent locator service that can tap into Social Security numbers, Department of Motor Vehicles records, unemployment rosters, and other databases to find missing child-support delinquents. Check with your state office of child-support collection, and you may just find him.

When I got divorced, the judge issued a court order for my spouse to pay child support. He hasn't paid. What's next?

Since the child support was ordered by the court, your spouse is in arrears. You can go back to court and request that a judgment be issued against your spouse for the amount owed.

My spouse is officially in arrears and is threatening to claim bankruptcy so he won't have to pay. Can he do that?

He can try, but he almost certainly won't succeed. Delinquent child support—along with back taxes and outstanding student loans—is a kind of debt that cannot be eliminated in a bankruptcy proceeding. All that filing bankruptcy can do for your spouse is delay the day of reckoning. While it is true that in the midst of a bankruptcy hearing all active attempts to collect a petitioner's debts must cease, when the proceeding is finished he will still owe back child support, and he will still have to pay.

MEDICAL DEBT

Medical bills can be some of the hardest bills to face. Not only can they be large, they can also represent a physical or emotional crisis for the patient or for a loved one. Here are a few guidelines for dealing with large medical debts.

I have recently undergone surgery. When I got the bills I was shocked. I found many charges that had broad categories but no itemization. How do I know what I am paying for?

Often, you don't know what you're paying for with a medical bill, and sometimes the hospital is hoping that you won't find out. Ask the hospital to itemize all charges, and it will comply.

My hospital bill is filled with codes, and I have no idea what they mean.

Call your hospital administrator and ask to review your bill with her. Ask her to translate every code on the bill for you. Then look it over again to be sure that you received the coded medications or services.

What is the likelihood that there are mistakes on my hospital bill?

The federal General Accounting Office estimates that the average hospital bill contains approximately $1,400 in errors. That is a lot of money. When you examine your bill, look for double charges, exorbitant charges for inexpensive items such as aspirin, and items or services that you didn't receive. If possible, while in the hospital, jot down medications you receive and services rendered, so that you have a record to compare with the bill when it comes.

I have gotten a huge medical bill, and I do not have the money to pay it. What can I do?

Depending on who sent the bill, call your hospital or your doctor. Explain the situation. In general, medical institutions tend to be less demanding and more lenient than a typical bank or credit card company, and many will accept a partial payment and/or suspend late fees and interest charges. If you stay in touch, chances are good your practitioner or hospital won't send the bill to a collection agency.

I am covered by insurance, but my insurance company will not pay my hospital bill, and the hospital is hounding me. Do I have to pay?

No, but you have to do some legwork. Make an appointment with the hospital administrator, show her copies of the claim forms you have submitted to the insurance company, and tell her that you cannot and will not pay the bill with your own resources. Many hospitals retain an ombudsman to help patients with insurers, so ask if one is available to help you.

Credit card companies have turned me down because of late payments reflected on my credit report. Most of these charges are related to an illness I had last year, and my HMO was supposed to pay them. The credit bureaus refuse to remove them. Help!

Unfortunately, this is a problem that's becoming commonplace. If I were you, I would write to the Federal Trade Commission, *www.ftc.gov,* to complain. If more and more people do this, maybe the FTC will act. But don't blame the credit bureau entirely—often, it is hard to tell if a collection account springs from unpaid medical bills or from a delinquent health insurance payment.

After you write to the FTC, assemble all the information you can about your insurance benefits and submit this material to the collection agency. It might also be worthwhile to contact the doctor or the hospital in question and explain that your credit is in jeopardy. And it is always worthwhile to provide documentation and an explanation—brief and concise— to your credit bureau. This will help to provide assurance that this is a one-time-only problem.

If my medical debt is so large that I feel I will never be able to pay it, can I get rid of it if I claim bankruptcy?

Probably, but you should consult a lawyer and get advice about your specific case.

IRS DEBT

I owe the IRS $5,000 in back taxes. What are my options if I do not have the money to pay?
You have only one option, other than to pay in full, and your eligibility for it depends on your never before having been delinquent with tax payments. If this is true, and if you owe the IRS $25,000 or less, you automatically qualify for what is called an installment plan. With an installment plan, you pay back taxes in installments over a period of months or years. If you owe more than $25,000, you may still qualify, but you must fill out additional forms and may be assigned a revenue officer to oversee your account. If you have been in trouble with the IRS in the past, this is probably not an option. Otherwise, call your local IRS office.

I have been told that the IRS will sometimes take less than the full amount if you offer to pay in full. Is this true?
Yes, in some cases the IRS will settle for less than the full amount owed. The official term for this kind of settlement is "offer in compromise." With an offer in compromise, you make one lump-sum payment and your debt is forgiven. There's a minimum you must offer, so please check with the IRS about this and other restrictions. Bottom line: It's a possibility.

If I file for bankruptcy, will my IRS debt be eliminated?
In most cases, the answer is no. But filing a Chapter 13 bankruptcy can help you spread out your IRS payments over time, halt the accrual of interest charges and penalties, and sus-

pend collection efforts, the garnishment of your wages, and the enforcement of any liens. So although filing for bankruptcy usually won't wipe the slate clean, it can provide some breathing room.

The only time an IRS debt can be considered for elimination is when every single one of the following conditions has been met. Even then, there's no guarantee, so please check with your tax adviser.

1. The taxes that you currently owe were assessed at least 240 days before you filed for bankruptcy.
2. The taxes you currently owe are based on a tax return that was filed at least two years before you filed for bankruptcy.
3. The taxes you currently owe are based on a tax return that should have been filed at least three years before you filed for bankruptcy.
4. The taxes you currently owe are not the result of a fraudulent return or an effort on your part to evade tax collection.

PREVENTING DEBT FROM JOB LOSS

How do I prepare for a job layoff or other income loss?
To make sure you are always prepared for the unknown, the first thing you need to do *after* paying off your credit card debt is establish an emergency fund to pay your monthly living expenses while you're not working. I want you to have enough cash saved for at least eight months. Yes, that's right: eight whole months of expenses in savings. I no longer believe that

the three- to six-month time frame that has traditionally been recommended for a reserve fund is enough. For one thing, because the economy has changed and job layoffs have become more prevalent, the time it takes to find another job is getting longer and longer.

How much do I need to have saved for an emergency fund?

In setting up an emergency fund, the first problem you may encounter is not knowing how much it actually costs you per month to live. Suppose you bring home a monthly paycheck of $3,000. By the end of the month, it's all gone. You may think that is how much you need to live each month, but the truth is that you may be spending far more than that. This is why your credit card debt keeps rising. To find out how much you really do spend each month, please do the exercise below. I don't want you to guess or estimate, but to work from the real figures over the past year.

1. Go through your records and receipts for the last complete calendar year. This includes all checks, all credit card charges, and all ATM withdrawals and cash advances.
2. Make categories for each month, such as telephone, gasoline, food, utilities, vet bills, recreation fees, and babysitting. You will have to record *every expenditure* you made in those 12 months—if you no longer recall what it was for, put it under "miscellaneous."
3. After you've filled in all the categories for the entire 12 months, add up the total for each category.
4. For each category, divide by 12. This will give you the *average* amount you spend on each category per month.

5. Now add together the averages for every category. This will tell you what it costs you to live each month.

Keep in mind that you're doing this exercise to get an *average* amount you spend per month. There will be months when you spend less and months when you spend more. I want you to work from the average figure. Doing this exercise completely is one of the only ways you can really get a grip on the knowns of your life.

I find it impossible to save. How am I ever going to be able to set up an emergency fund for eight months' worth of expenses?

Well, my friend, if this is the case, the way for you to create an emergency fund is simply to take every extra penny you have, put it into a money-market account, and *save it there*. You have to make a decision here. Which means more to you: having a Starbucks coffee this afternoon and going to the movies tonight, or knowing that you and your loved ones will be protected even if you lose your job or get sick? Doing what is right for you—including making sure you'll have what you need in any situation—may mean giving up what you *want* right now, to pay for what you *need* later on. I hope you decide to do this, for you'll be amazed at how much control over your life you will feel with your emergency fund standing behind you.

While you are figuring out how to save for an emergency fund, here are some actions you can take. If you own a home with equity in it, you might want to establish an equity line of credit with the amount that you need to get you through those eight months of expenses—just in case.

Equity is the value of your home above and beyond what you owe to the mortgage company. If your house has appreciated in value since you purchased it, your equity, or cash value, in that home has increased as well. You might be able to use that cash as an emergency fund through an equity line of credit that you arrange for with a bank or mortgage company. If you are eligible, the lender of this equity line of credit will provide you with a checkbook that will let you write checks against the equity in your home. You will pay interest on only the portion of the funds that you actually use. Equity credit is a good backup to have as you build up an actual emergency fund, but it must be kept safe and used only for a situation in which you have a loss of income. To do otherwise would put you in jeopardy and break this law of money.

If you do not own a home or if your home currently has no equity in it—or even if it does—I want you to take another step toward having the money you will need in case of an emergency. Here's what to do. Apply for and take out one or more credit cards with available credit limits that cover the amount that you will need for your eight months of living expenses. If you cannot get credit limits that cover the entire amount, come as close as you can. If the unforeseen happens—if you become ill or lose your job—you can use this credit by taking cash advances. That said, again, *please* do not use this money to incur debts if you are currently employed. That would be plunging yourself back into the unknown, big-time.

The time to set up both an equity line of credit and emergency credit card lines is when you *do* have a job and income is coming in. If you ever do suffer an unforeseen crisis, such as a job layoff or illness, and you are without an income stream, it will be very difficult to set up these credit lines. Do it now.

I have been offered a voluntary severance. Should I take it?

This is what you need to consider: When you're offered a severance package, it normally gives you one to two weeks of pay for every year you have worked for a company. When you hear this, you may think, "Well, all right, they're going to give me $30,000 without my having to work for it; that sounds like a good deal. I'll take it." The question is: Will you get the whole $30,000 to put in your pocket? The answer is no. For tax purposes, severance is considered income, just like your paycheck—and in addition to federal, state, and local income taxes, you'll have to pay Social Security and Medicare taxes on that money. By the time you get your check, you'll be lucky to get $20,000.

Still, if you think you can quickly find another job, this might look like found money to you. Be careful here. You have to understand that, if you are in a recession or there is a tight job market in your field, finding another job might not be as easy as you think. You have to run through these possibilities in your mind, along with your financial calculations. What would happen if you could not find another job—an equally good job—for eight months, a year, or a year and a half? What would you do for income once the severance runs out? Are you willing to spend your emergency fund, if you have it in place?

If you're considering taking a voluntary severance package offered by your company, please ask for a complete rundown of everything that's included in the package, especially company-paid health insurance and the right to keep your health insurance at your own expense under COBRA laws. (COBRA, short for the Consolidated Omnibus Budget Reconciliation Act of 1986, guarantees you the right to continue in your former employer's group health plan for up to 18 months, at your own expense, even if you voluntarily leave a job.) Also ask whether you'll be eligible for unemployment insurance, should you need it. And please test the employment waters before you accept a severance offer.

BANKRUPTCY

Who is bankruptcy for, exactly?

Bankruptcy is for anyone who can't pay back all his or her debts. There are different forms of bankruptcy for different circumstances. Two of the most common are Chapter 7, in which all your debts (except student loans and taxes) are excused, and Chapter 13, in which filing for bankruptcy gives you the opportunity to work out repayment schedules that are fair to you and your creditors, while protecting your assets from being seized by your creditors. In 2005, Congress passed a bankruptcy reform law that makes it much more difficult to file for Chapter 7 bankruptcy, the kind that allows you to entirely eliminate most debts; many more debtors would now have to file for Chapter 13 bankruptcy, where most debts—including credit card debts—must be repaid on a schedule worked out by a court. Still, bankruptcy can offer some debtors breathing room and a chance at reestablishing a responsible and less stressful financial life.

What is involuntary bankruptcy?

Involuntary bankruptcy is a situation in which your creditors, rather than you, file the petition for bankruptcy.

I feel terrible about considering bankruptcy, but years of unplanned medical bills have forced me to this point!

Terrible things—illness, death, natural disaster, or an unforeseen financial blow—can happen to anyone. Bankruptcy laws take this into consideration—in fact, they exist to help people in situations like these. If you've faced great adversity, you should be permitted to start over again, and declaring bankruptcy can help.

I'm deeply in debt, and I'm thinking of filing for bankruptcy. If I do, will the consequences be significant?

Filing for bankruptcy has serious, long-term emotional as well as financial consequences. It is not referred to as the "ten-year mistake" for nothing! I want to emphasize that bankruptcy is not to be taken lightly. I consider it an option to be acted on reluctantly, after much thought, when—and only when—there is no other way out.

What kinds of questions should I ask myself before filing for bankruptcy?

Filing for bankruptcy may help you to resolve your debt problem, but it won't help those to whom you owe money. Imagine how you'd feel if someone who owed you a lot of money sent a letter saying, "Sorry, I'm bankrupt; I won't be paying you back." Ask yourself these questions: To whom do you owe money? Credit card companies? Friends? Businesses? Will you have to see or deal with any of these people or institutions after you file for bankruptcy, and if so, how will that make you feel? What financial hardship, if any, will you cause for others if you take such a step? Is there absolutely no other way for you to climb out of debt, little by little, with work and determination?

I'm in debt because of overspending on my credit cards. I really don't owe a lot, but I'm thinking of filing for bankruptcy so I can start over. Is this a good idea?

Not under the new laws. Chances are, if your income is high enough, you will be obliged to pay back your credit card debts.

Even if the debts will be forgiven, however, you must consider issues that go beyond your immediate financial difficulties. Please remember this: If you do not pay your debts, someone else will have to. In the case of debt to a bank or a credit card company, the institution in question will have to absorb the loss you incur and will probably, in one form or another, pass that loss along to the rest of us. For example, your bankruptcy could affect the scoring system that credit bureaus use, which might mean that someone you don't know will be turned down for credit.

Declaring bankruptcy is one of the most important financial steps you will ever consider taking. It will bring a whole new set of complications and difficulties into your already complicated and difficult life.

First, think about what declaring bankruptcy will do to your credit report. If you declare bankruptcy, you will find it extremely difficult, if not impossible, to get credit. It will be difficult to rent an apartment, buy a house, or rent a car without a credit card. It is very likely that you will lose property you had counted on keeping for a long time. Future job opportunities may be affected too, which could lead to future financial problems. And in many cases, someone else—perhaps a friend, a spouse, or a cosigner—will be saddled with your debts.

Before filing for bankruptcy please understand the magnitude of what you are about to do. Please understand the sacrifice you are making, as well as what you will gain. Please understand what you are asking of others. Finally, if you decide that this is the only way out, I hope you will start over from a place of pride and courage, not one of shame.

Is there a minimum amount of debt you must have before filing for bankruptcy?

No, there is not. An attorney I know sees people who file for Chapter 7 and Chapter 13 bankruptcy with debts of as little as $5,000. I wouldn't recommend this, since your debts should be large enough to justify the legal expenses you will incur as well as the long-term consequences of bankruptcy.

Should I contact a lawyer before I consider filing for bankruptcy?

Definitely. Before you do anything, check with an attorney who can explain the current state of the law, the pros and cons of filing for bankruptcy, and the differences between the kinds of bankruptcy.

Can I be fired for filing bankruptcy?

Legally, no.

A friend of mine who once declared bankruptcy recently applied for a job. When her prospective employer looked at her credit report, he turned her down on the basis of the bankruptcy, even though that was 13 years ago. Is this legal?

It may not be legal, but it's a fact of life. Think about it: 1.4 million people claim bankruptcy every year. It's virtually impossible for credit bureaus to keep up with the recordkeeping required to make sure all the negative information is removed when the time's up in each and every case. So it's up to you to see that your information is up-to-date and accurately reflects your credit standing.

After many years of struggle, my husband is declaring bankruptcy. Should he file alone, or should we file together?

The answer to your question depends on many factors, including whether or not you own your property together and, if so, what type of property it is. If you file together, you will erase your own debts, your husband's debts, and all your jointly held marital debts. If your husband files by himself, his individual debts will be wiped out, and so will his share of your joint debts. But that still leaves you liable for your share of your joint debts. Further, in community-property states, where husbands and wives equally own all property earned or received during the marriage, your share in the property is considered part of the bankruptcy estate even if you don't file jointly with your husband during his bankruptcy.

What about property I owned alone, before my marriage?

Property you own separately is not affected by your husband's bankruptcy, unless you've put him on the title or commingled those assets with him.

TYPES OF BANKRUPTCY

There are several kinds of personal bankruptcy, but Chapter 7 and Chapter 13 are by far the most common. Chapter 12 bankruptcy applies to farmers, and Chapter 11 bankruptcy is often used by major corporations that cannot repay their debts.

CHAPTER 7 BANKRUPTCY

What is Chapter 7 bankruptcy?

Until recently, Chapter 7 bankruptcy has been the most common type of bankruptcy. Under Chapter 7, a court-appointed trustee assembles all your assets, sells them for cash, and then allocates and distributes the money to your creditors. You can hold on to any assets that are exempt under federal law and/or the laws of the state you live in. Basically, Chapter 7 is a way for you to erase most of your debts—but not without giving up some of your property.

What qualifications must I meet to file for Chapter 7 bankruptcy?

You must meet an income qualification. According to the new federal law, if over the course of the next five years you are expected to have enough income to repay 25 percent or more of your unsecured debts, including credit card debt, child support debt, medical debt, and IRS debt, you would be *unable* to file for Chapter 7 bankruptcy and would be steered to Chapter 13 instead. You will also have to get credit counseling with an agency approved by the United States Trustee's office before filing, and additional counseling once your bankruptcy case is over.

How do I go about filing for Chapter 7?

First, you must fill out a number of forms and applications listing your income, the amounts and kinds of your debts, and what assets you possess—house, land, car—above and beyond your debts. (You can find these forms in books about bankruptcy published by Nolo Press.) You must divulge complete financial information in a petition for Chapter 7 bankruptcy. If you forget a debt, or leave one out, it may not be erased. Even worse, if you fail to list all your assets you could later be liable for fraud.

After I finish filling out the forms and applications, what happens?

After completing the paperwork, you file a petition for bankruptcy with the court (for a fee), and a court date will be set.

Your creditors will be informed that you have filed for Chapter 7. You will then be appointed an impartial trustee, a person charged by the court to oversee your bankruptcy plan.

How much will filing for Chapter 7 bankruptcy cost?

The fee for an individual filing will be about $160 to $175. For a couple filing jointly, the fee can range from $500 to $1,500. If you can't pay this amount all at once, you can pay it in installments. In addition, you should hire an attorney. If you cannot afford the services of an attorney, look in your phone book under free or discount legal services. Legally you can always represent yourself at your hearing, but it is never a good idea to act as your own lawyer.

Once I have filed for bankruptcy, will creditors and collection agencies stop breathing down my neck?

In most cases, yes. The filing of your petition automatically stays, or stops, your creditors from garnishing your wages, emptying your checking or savings account, pursuing you, or attempting to sue you for nonpayment. But this should not be the main reason you file for bankruptcy.

What are the responsibilities of the court-appointed trustee?

The trustee is responsible for overseeing all your financial affairs after you have petitioned for Chapter 7. A month or so after you have filed, you will attend a short hearing attended by your creditors and your trustee. This hearing is a question-and-answer period in which the creditors are given a good look at what you own and at the extent of your debts. After the hearing, the trustee will arrange to sell off your nonexempt property. This could include some equity in your home and your car, a portion of your property, and a certain amount of cash. Your trustee will then divide the proceeds among your lenders and creditors.

Are all debts considered the same in bankruptcy court?
No. By law, debts are divided into two categories: discharge-able and non-dischargeable. A court will determine how the law applies to your debts.

What kinds of debts can I get rid of during a Chapter 7 bankruptcy hearing?
After the bankruptcy proceeding, you will not have to pay what is known as dischargeable debt. The most common kinds of dischargeable debt in a Chapter 7 hearing include back rent you owe a landlord; outstanding utility bills, including gas, electricity, and phone; some court judgments against you (but not child and/or spousal support, which cannot be dis-charged); credit card, charge card, department store card, and gasoline card bills; documented loans from your friends or family; any outstanding legal or medical bills; and most, if not all, unsecured loans ("unsecured" here means debts that have no collateral attached to them).

What debts cannot be charged off in Chapter 7 bank-ruptcy?
You are responsible for what's called non-dischargeable debt, including any loan that was issued, funded, guaranteed, or insured by a government entity or a nonprofit corporation (such as taxes, government fines, all student loans, and Federal Housing Administration loans). You are also liable for any debt that the court determines you incurred due to irresponsible behavior or that was incurred long before you got into general financial trouble. Also, if you bought expensive items or took out a cash advance right before filing for bankruptcy, these debts will be considered non-dischargeable. You may be respon-sible for any secured debts—i.e., debts with collateral—and any debts arising out of trouble with the law. If you were sued

for personal injury while you were driving drunk, or if you owe any debts because of traffic violations, fraud, larceny, embezzlement, assault, or libel, you will still be responsible for these debts after a bankruptcy proceeding. You will also be liable for any alimony or child-support debt. Your non-dischargeable debts will be treated as if no bankruptcy had been filed, so a creditor can seek payment by any legal means.

What property will I lose if I file for Chapter 7?

The types of property you stand to lose (called "nonexempt" property) depend on the laws of your state. Among other things, however, you could very well lose (if applicable) your second home, your second car, any stock or bond certificates, CDs, money-market funds, and any valuable collections (stamps, coins) or heirlooms, as well as part of your marital estate.

What is "exempt" property?

Exempt property is property that you get to keep after you file for a Chapter 7 bankruptcy. There are state exemptions and federal exemptions, and you can choose under which auspices you want to file after considering which offers you a higher allowance. Typically, you can keep your home up to a certain dollar value (in California, for example, the state exemption for a homestead allowance can range from $50,000 to 150,000), your clothes, your furniture and appliances, your personal effects, your jewelry, your retirement plans and life insurance, and your income from Social Security, disability, unemployment, welfare, and/or alimony. If you bought your car with an auto loan, then it is considered a secured debt that cannot be discharged unless you give the car back; in other words, if you want to keep your car, you'll have to keep paying your car loan. There are cases in which you may wish to "reaffirm" that debt.

Are my IRA and 401(k) protected during a Chapter 7 filing?

401(k) plans, company pension plans, and other ERISA-qualified plans are generally exempted from the bankruptcy estate. Individual IRA accounts are not ERISA-qualified plans, but in some states IRAs may be exempted, too.

What is a reaffirmation?

Depending on your financial and personal circumstances, you may want to keep possession of a piece of property you feel you cannot do without. If so, you may want to look into the possibility of reaffirming the debt. This means that in spite of the bankruptcy proceedings, you agree to pay all or a portion of the money to the creditor in question. In return, the creditor promises that he will not repossess your car, or whatever else it is that you are anxious to hold on to. Before you take this step, however, I would strongly advise that you contact an attorney to make sure you know all your rights.

I don't have any assets to hand over to the trustee. Can I still file for Chapter 7?

Yes. In fact, most Chapter 7 cases involve persons who have few, if any, assets to liquidate to satisfy their creditors' claims.

What is an insolvency period?

The insolvency period is the three-month period before you filed for bankruptcy. This is also known as a look-back period. A trustee or a judge will examine your payments during this period to see whether you showed preference to some creditors. For example, did you repay your aunt Milly the $500 you owed her but claim poverty when Visa and American Express asked for what you owed them? If it is found that you engaged in avoidable preference, the money will be returned to the court and distributed proportionally among your creditors.

My property has been liquidated and the proceeds distributed. Now what?

Now the court will arrange for a final hearing. At that point, it will usually discharge your remaining debts.

What does "discharge your debts" mean?

Discharging your debts is another way of saying your dischargeable debts are over and done with—history. You no longer owe your creditors anything, and they are forbidden by law from trying to collect any unpaid percentage of the original debt. You are legally off the hook. Usually, under Chapter 7, debt is discharged within six months, often within half that time. You'll probably be informed by mail of this discharge.

Can a discharge ever be revoked?

In certain circumstances, yes, but it's rare. A discharge can be revoked if for some reason the discharge was obtained fraudulently, or if the debtor failed to disclose any property during his financial disclosure.

Are there any grounds for denying a discharge?

Again, it's rare, but the court can deny a discharge if the debtor has not kept adequate financial records, if he has perjured himself before the court, or if he has concealed, destroyed, or failed to note any property that because of the bankruptcy petition is now in the court's jurisdiction.

A creditor of mine is trying to collect a debt that the court has discharged. What should I do?

In some cases, this is considered civil contempt. Discharge is permanent. File a motion with the court that handled your bankruptcy filing, reporting the creditor's action and requesting that your case be reopened to look into this matter.

Can filing a Chapter 7 bankruptcy stop a bank from foreclosing on my house?

It depends on your state's laws. Please check. Filing a Chapter 13 bankruptcy will postpone foreclosure indefinitely, as long as you resume making monthly payments on your mortgage. Check your state's laws to find out if personal residences are exempted from liquidation during bankruptcy.

CHAPTER 13 BANKRUPTCY

What is Chapter 13 bankruptcy?

Chapter 13 bankruptcy is for people who are employed or are earning a regular income from a pension, an annuity, or some other source but who are unable to pay the full extent of their debts. Chapter 13 is a repayment plan executed under the supervision of a court, and it involves an agreement on your part to pay back a portion of the money you owe, based on the amount of your income and the size of your debts. Because of the new bankruptcy law, more people who once would have filed Chapter 7 bankruptcy are being directed into Chapter 13 bankruptcy.

Do I file for Chapter 13 in the same way I would file for Chapter 7?

Yes. You fill out the same papers, pay a filing fee—usually about $274—and get a court-appointed trustee. You will also need to attend credit counseling with an agency approved by the United States Trustee's office. But, in addition, you have to submit to the court a plan for the repayment of your unsecured debts, including credit card debt. The court will either accept or reject this plan. In the case of secured debts, you agree to pay back, at the minimum, the amount of the claim that the creditor is willing to accept, or else you agree to surrender the collateral.

Do I pay the money directly to the trustee?

Yes. After you have filled out a form listing your assets and income and set up a confirmation hearing, your court-appointed trustee will begin making payments to all your creditors according to the terms of the court-approved repayment schedule.

Do all my debts count here, or are there exceptions, as is the case with Chapter 7?

Certain debts cannot be renegotiated in a Chapter 13 bankruptcy, including child support, alimony, and local, state, and federal taxes. You also continue to be responsible for any and all regular mortgage payments. If you miss a payment, the lender can have your home removed from under the bankruptcy and foreclose on it.

How long does Chapter 13 last?

It can take three, sometimes four years before your debts are discharged. As with Chapter 7, you will need to attend credit counseling after your case, as well.

Can anybody file for Chapter 13?

If your secured debt is less than $922,975 and your unsecured debt is less than $307,675 (whether you are single or married), you may be eligible to file for Chapter 13 (these figures are accurate as of the year 2006). Stockbrokers and commodity brokers are legally prohibited from filing for Chapter 13.

What if I can't keep up with my Chapter 13 repayment plan? Does this mean I have to file for Chapter 7?

If you find that you cannot honor your repayment schedule under Chapter 13—if you lost your job, fell ill, or got a divorce, for example—you should contact your court-appointed trustee immediately. Depending on your situation, the trustee may be able to get the court to cut you some slack, particularly if your inability to repay your debts is only temporary. If it looks like it could be long-term, the court has several options: It could alter your repayment schedule to reflect your new circumstances, it could discharge your remaining debts on the basis of hardship, or it could convert your Chapter 13 bankruptcy to a Chapter 7 bankruptcy.

A Comparison of Chapter 7 and Chapter 13

Which is better, Chapter 7 or Chapter 13 bankruptcy?
I think you mean, "Which is less bad?" The answer to this depends on your financial situation. Each form of bankruptcy, Chapter 7 and Chapter 13, has its pros and cons. If you have really serious financial problems, no doubt you will prefer a straight Chapter 7 proceeding, if you can get one.

What are the relative advantages of Chapter 7 bankruptcy?
From start to finish, from the date you file to the date your debts are discharged, Chapter 7 is faster to complete than Chapter 13. And it gives people a "fresh start" (though not without a lot of drawbacks, as I've mentioned). In a Chapter 7 bankruptcy, the amount of dischargeable, unsecured debt, such as credit card debt, that you can erase from your life is unlimited, provided all assets and debts were declared and there is no suspicion of fraud in your filing.

What are the relative disadvantages of Chapter 7 bankruptcy?
The disadvantages of Chapter 7 bankruptcy are numerous. First of all, you have to give up your nonexempt property—

including, say, a second home or second car—hand it over to the court, and allow it to be sold. Even after you file under Chapter 7, some of your debts may survive (those deemed secured and non-dischargeable, such as a car loan, and those that a creditor feels were incurred with the intention to defraud the creditor), and with respect to those debts you can still be approached by collection agencies. If a friend or a family member cosigned any of your loans, he or she will now be stuck with your debt—which is not at all nice. Once you have filed for Chapter 7, it is very difficult to reverse the process. And, of course, like any bankruptcy, a Chapter 7 bankruptcy will not look good on your credit history.

What are the relative advantages of Chapter 13 bankruptcy?

The main advantage of Chapter 13 is that you get to keep all your property, whether it is exempt or nonexempt. Your creditors can't garnish your wages or send collectors after you, and you are protected against foreclosure. In Chapter 13, you are allowed to separate your debts by class. Different classes of creditors are due different percentages of payment. You also have a lot longer to pay back your debts than you do under Chapter 7 (remember, not all of your debts may be dischargeable under Chapter 7). And if you arrange to pay back your debts in full, your creditors can't go after anyone who has cosigned a loan.

What are the relative disadvantages of filing Chapter 13?

Your total debt, secured and unsecured, has to be under $1,230,650, as noted earlier (less than $922,975 of secured debt and $307,675 of unsecured debt). You pay back your debts out of your own income, which can tie up your income for a long time. If debts survive after your bankruptcy is closed, you have to keep paying back those debts. You could find yourself in this situation for many years, which could have a serious effect on your future income.

What are the tax obligations of a person who files for bankruptcy?

Your tax obligations will depend on whether you have filed under Chapter 7 or Chapter 13. If you file under Chapter 7, this petition creates a separate, taxable bankruptcy estate consisting of all assets that belonged to you before the filing date. Your trustee is responsible for preparing and filing any taxes attached this estate. You, the individual debtor, are responsible for any taxes that are not connected to the estate (i.e., your income taxes). If you file under Chapter 13, this petition does not create a separate taxable estate, and you continue to pay taxes as you did before you filed for bankruptcy.

How will my bankruptcy affect my credit report? Am I wiping the slate clean?

"Wiping the slate clean" is a misleading phrase because your credit report will show, for seven to ten years after the fact, that you filed for bankruptcy. This puts all lenders on notice that you are a risky person to lend money to.

If I claim bankruptcy, does that mean I will not be able to get another credit card?

Years ago, that is exactly what it would have meant. Nowadays, however, some credit card companies actually seek out people who have claimed bankruptcy and offer them credit cards. "What's wrong with that?" you may ask. Well, once you have claimed bankruptcy, you cannot do so again for a period of years. Within that time, if you get into trouble with your credit cards, there is no way you can get out of paying your debts.

How often can I file for bankruptcy?

I wouldn't make a habit out of it! Legally, however, you can file for Chapter 7 bankruptcy once every six years. Most Chapter 13 plans have three- to five-year payouts, so while technically you can file for Chapter 13 as often as needed, it is unlikely you'll be filing more often than the term of your payment schedule.

ADDITIONAL RESOURCES

CORPORATE CREDIT CARDS

Here is the contact information for the five largest charge and credit card companies:

American Express
(800) 528-4800
www.americanexpress.com

Diners Club
(800) 234-6377
www.dinersclub.com

Discover
(800) 347-2683
www.discovercard.com

MasterCard
(800) 424-7787
www.mastercard.com

Visa
(800) VISA-911
www.visa.com

To shop for the card that best fits your needs, compare rates and services, and access easy-to-understand credit and debt information, please visit *www.bankrate.com*.

REMOVE YOUR NAME FROM MAILING AND TELEMARKETING LISTS

Contact the Direct Marketing Association's Mail, E-Mail, and Telephone Preference services at the following addresses:

DMA Mail Preference Service
(212) 768-7277
www.dmaconsumers.org/offmailinglist.html

DMA Telephone Preference Service
(212) 768-7277
www.dmaconsumers.org/offtelephonelist.html

DMA E-Mail Preference Service
(212) 768-7277
www.dmaconsumers.org/consumers/optoutform_emps.shtml

To remove your name from the three major credit bureaus' pre-screening or other marketing lists, you may contact each credit bureau individually (see information below), or call their toll-free number, (888) 5OPT-OUT, to reach the National Opt-Out Center.

Equifax
Equifax Credit Information Services, Inc.
P.O. Box 740241
Atlanta, GA 30374
(800) 685-1111 (for general inquiries)

Experian (formerly TRW)
Experian Consumer Services
901 West Bond Street
Lincoln, NE 68521

Trans Union Corporation
TransUnion LLC's Name Removal Option
P.O. Box 97328
Jackson, MS 39288-7328

To add your phone number to the National Do Not Call Registry, contact the Federal Trade commission at the following phone number or website:

National Do Not Call Registry
(888) 382-1222
www.donotcall.gov

CREDIT CARDS TO
EARN AIRLINE MILES

Southwest Rapid Rewards/VISA
(800) 792-8472

Delta SkyMiles/Am Exp Centurion
(800) SKYMILE

Continental Airlines/Chase Manhattan
(800) 377-0601

United Airlines Mileage Plus/Chase
(800) 537-7783

USAirways Dividend Miles/Bank of America
(800) 341-7568

ADDITIONAL RESOURCES

American Airlines Citibank AAdvantage
(800) 456-4277

Northwest Airlines WorldPerks/US Bank
(800) 360-2900

To shop for the card that best fits your needs, compare rates and services, and access easy-to-understand credit and debt information, please visit *www.bankrate.com.*

CREDIT CARDS WITH LOW INTEREST RATES

Pulaski Bank & Trust Co.
(800) 980-2265

Amalgamated Bank of Chicago
(800) 723-0303

MBNA America Bank
(866) 253-0640

5 Star Bank
(800) 776-2265

Blue from American Express
(800) 641-2400

Orchard Bank
www.hsbapply.com/start/orchardbank

Household Bank, FSB
(800) 685-9080

ADDITIONAL RESOURCES

COUNSELING SERVICES

National Foundation for Credit Counseling Service (NFCC)
You can reach NFCC at (800) 388-2227 or visit their website, *www.nfcc.org*, to find a credit counselor in your area.

The Association of Credit and Collection Professionals
(952) 926-6547
www.acainternational.org

Debtors Anonymous
Debtors Anonymous General Services
P.O. Box 920888
Needham, MA 02492-0009
(781) 453-2743 (all calls are confidential)
www.debtorsanonymous.org

CREDIT REPORTS AND SCORES

Here are the addresses, phone numbers, and websites of the big three credit bureaus, as well as the address of the Federal Trade Commission.

Equifax Credit Information Services, Inc.
P.O. Box 740241
Atlanta, GA 30374
(800) 685-1111
www.equifax.com

Experian
P.O. Box 2002
Allen, TX 75013
(888) 397-3742
www.experian.com

ADDITIONAL RESOURCES

TransUnion LLC
Consumer Disclosure Center
P.O. Box 2000
Chester, PA 19022
(877) 322-8228 to get your credit report
(800) 916-8800 to ask questions about your report
www.tuc.com

MyFICO
www.myfico.com
For credit report and credit score information.

Federal Trade Commission, Main Office
6th Street & Pennsylvania Avenue, NW
Washington, DC 20580
www.ftc.gov

LOANS

For information on Perkins, Stafford, and PLUS loans, contact:

U.S. Department of Education
400 Maryland Avenue, SW
Washington, DC 20202-0498
(800) USA-LEARN
www.ed.gov

To report harassment by debt collectors, contact the Deputy Director of Debt Collections at (202) 708-4766. If harassment continues, call the Policy Development Division of the Loan Branch of the Department of Education, (202) 708-8242.

BOOKS

Chapter 13 Bankruptcy: Repay Your Debts, by Robin Leonard
Attorney Leonard is back with a comprehensive and trustworthy guide to the ins and outs of filing for Chapter 13 bankruptcy. You can write or call Nolo Press at 930 Parker Street, Berkeley, CA 94710, (800) 992-6656, or access their website at *www.nolo.com.*

How to File for Chapter 7 Bankruptcy, by Stephen Elias, Albin Renauer, and Robin Leonard
The best guide out there to filing for Chapter 7 bankruptcy.

Money Troubles: Legal Strategies to Cope with Your Debts, by Robin Leonard
A comprehensive step-by-step guide to facing and dealing head-on with your debts.

The Ultimate Credit Handbook: How to Double Your Credit, Cut Your Debt, and Have a Lifetime of Great Credit, by Gerri Detweiler
The definitive and most up-to-date resource for getting, keeping, and managing credit.

INDEX

ABOUT SUZE ORMAN

SUZE ORMAN has been called "a force in the world of personal finance" and a "one-woman financial advice powerhouse" by *USA Today*. A two-time Emmy® Award–winning television show host, *New York Times* best-selling author, magazine and online columnist, writer-producer, and motivational speaker, Suze is undeniably America's most recognized personal finance expert.

Suze has written five consecutive *New York Times* best sellers— *The Money Book for the Young, Fabulous & Broke*; *The Laws of Money, The Lessons of Life*; *The Road to Wealth*; *The Courage to Be Rich*; and *The 9 Steps to Financial Freedom*—as well as the national best sellers *Suze Orman's Financial Guidebook* and *You've Earned It, Don't Lose It*. Her most recent book, *Women & Money*, was published by Spiegel & Grau in February 2007. A newspaper column, also called "Women & Money," syndicated by Universal Press Syndicate, began in January 2007. Additionally, she has created *Suze Orman's FICO Kit*, *Suze Orman's Will & Trust*

Kit, Suze Orman's Insurance Kit, The Ask Suze Library System, and *Suze Orman's Ultimate Protection Portfolio.*

Suze has written, coproduced, and hosted five PBS specials based on her *New York Times* best-selling books, She is the single most successful fundraiser in the history of public television, and recently won her second Daytime Emmy® Award in the category of Outstanding Service Show Host. Suze won her first Emmy® in 2004, in the same category.

Suze is a contributing editor to *O, The Oprah Magazine* and *O at Home* and has a biweekly column, "Money Matters," on Yahoo! Finance. Suze hosts her own award-winning national CNBC-TV show, *The Suze Orman Show,* which airs every Saturday night, as well as *Financial Freedom Hour* on QVC television.

Suze has been honored with three American Women in Radio and Television (AWRT) Gracie Allen Awards. This award recognizes the nation's best radio, television, and cable programming for, by, and about women. In 2003, Suze garnered her first Gracie for *The Suze Orman Show* in the National/Network/Syndication Talk Show category. She won her second and third Gracies in the Individual Achievement: Program Host category in 2005 and 2006.

Profiled in *Worth* magazine's 100th issue as among those "who have revolutionized the way America thinks about money," Suze also was named one of *Smart Money* magazine's top thirty "Power Brokers," defined as those who have most influenced the mutual fund industry and affected our money, in 1999. A 2003 inductee into the Books for a Better Life (BBL) Award Hall of Fame in recognition of her ongoing contributions to self-improvement, Suze previously received the 1999 BBL Motivational Book Award for *The Courage to Be Rich.* As a tribute to her continuing involvement, in 2002 the organization established the Suze Orman First Book Award to honor a first-time author of a self-improvement book in any category. She received a 2003 Crossing Borders Award from the Feminist Press. The award recognizes a distinguished group of women who not only have excelled in remarkable careers but also have shown great courage, vision, and conviction by forging new places for women in their respective fields. In 2002, Suze was selected as one of five distinguished recipients of the prestigious TJFR Group News Luminaries Award, which honors lifetime achievement in business journalism.

A sought-after motivational speaker, Suze has lectured widely throughout the United States, South Africa, and Asia to audiences of up to fifty thousand people, often appearing alongside individuals such as Colin Powell, Rudy Giuliani, Jerry Lewis, Steve Forbes, and Donald Trump. She has been featured in almost every major publication in the United States and has appeared numerous times on *The View*, *Larry King Live*, and *The Oprah Winfrey Show*.

A Certified Financial Planner®, Suze directed the Suze Orman Financial Group from 1987 to 1997, served as vice president of investments for Prudential Bache Securities from 1983 to 1987, and from 1980 to 1983 was an account executive at Merrill Lynch. Prior to that, she worked as a waitress at the Buttercup Bakery in Berkeley, California, from 1973 to 1980.